Past the Sky's Rim:

THE ELDER SCROLLS
AND THEOLOGY

GRAY MATTER BOOKS

Past the Sky's Rim:

THE ELDER SCROLLS

AND THEOLOGY

EDITED BY JOSHUA WISE

GRAY MATTER BOOKS / LOS ANGELES

ISBN: 9780988930520

Bulk copies of this book can be ordered by contacting:

Gray Matter Books
8033 Sunset Blvd. #164
Hollywood, CA. 90046
info@graymatterbooks.com

To my wife, Sara, who endures both my theology and video games with grace. And to my parents who both purchased my first console and sent me to Catechism. These things have born fruit.

CONTENTS

INTRODUCTION

The great 19th-Century preacher, writer, and servant of Christ, George MacDonald spoke of two faculties of the human being that are the most like God. In MacDonald's understanding, the most divine element of the human person is the will, which MacDonald rooted in the very being of God. It was by the will that the Father and the Son live in perfect love. By the will, the human being obeyed God in imitation of and obedience to the Incarnate Son. God, in Godself, is imaged in the human willing.

But it is in the imagination that the human being was most like God in God's acts *ad extra*, beyond Godself. In the act of imagining, the man or woman images the living God in God's creative act. The imagination unpacks the teachings and meanings of Jesus, the most perfect outworking of divine and human life. In our dreaming, we are like our Heavenly Father.

This book of theology and imagination is a love letter, both to that Heavenly Father and to the relatively new medium of video games. It is the working out of an idea, a principle of theology that the Son is the image of the Living Father and that the world is made through the Son in perfect agreement with the free will of the Father and, thus, as an image of the Father. Among the many things made on this earth, humanity was made in the image of God, perhaps to be the great ministers of God to the rest of creation. We, as images of our creator, work out in our creation that original image and pattern which the Son of God both is and sets forth. It is a theology, an anthropology of the divine image, that convinces many of us that the work of human hands, though fallen and in desperate need of resurrection and the purifying fire of God, still may hold within it the image of the Good Father of Jesus Christ.

Throughout human history, the elements of art have each been submitted in one form or another to the eye of theology. The narrative, the painting, the sculpture and the symphony have all received the attention of theological minds. So we turn ours to the medium of video games, of interactive narrative and play. We consider how the stories we tell are reflections of our world, a broken image itself, and how we might think more deeply about them and learn from them. We here consider, as St. Irenaeus might put it, a defaced image of the king.

Why **The Elder Scrolls**

This volume, which is my incredible privilege to edit and contribute to, takes for its "text" the amazing series of games that Bethesda Softworks has produced, *The Elder Scrolls*. It is a series that began in 1994, and as of April 2014, is venturing into the Massively Multiplayer Online space. The games, *Arena* (1994), *Daggerfall* (1996), *Battlespire* (1997), *Redguard* (1998), *Morrowind* (2002), *Oblivion* (2006), *Skyrim* (2011) and *The Elder Scrolls* Online (planned for 2014) have spanned decades of our time and centuries of game time. As well, the lesser known games, *Stormhold*, *Dawnstar* and *Shadow Key*, met the hunger for more Elder Scrolls even on mobile platforms. It is a world rich in history, mythology and religion. As will be said multiple times in this work, it is a world that surpasses most fantasy worlds and rivals the Olympian heights of the mythology of Middle Earth.

There are many books on "the Theology of X." For good or bad, theologians are considering the popular media we consume and holding it up to the scrutiny of their education and understanding. Classes have been taught at Yale about Harry Potter and religion.[1] We are a people fascinated by the intersection of those things that have stood the test of millennia and those that are just bubbling to the surface of culture. *The Elder Scrolls* sits close to the bubbling edge of culture, though relative to passing fads it has staying power, as it has lasted nearly two decades, only gaining in popularity. It is also especially suited for the kind of treatment this book offers. Many games demonstrate an implicit theology, but *The Elder Scrolls* has a blatant explicit theology as well. And, unlike many fantasy games that merely take the names of things from real-world mythologies, *The Elder Scrolls* rather takes themes and meanings from Christian, Gnostic, Norse and other belief systems. Where other stories might think that Nithhog was a good name for a sword, *The Elder Scrolls* ignores the name, but keeps the idea of the serpent who heralds the end of the world.

The Essays

Our volume attempts to come at the "text" of *The Elder Scrolls* from many different directions.

Joshua Gonnerman's "Trinity and Tribunal" begins the book by looking into the concepts of three divine persons in one godhead in the lore of *Morrowind*, as well as the traditional Christian doctrines.

Matthew Frank's "As I Lay Dying: Witness and Death in *Morrowind*" considers the existential aspects of Morrowind, a first person solitary RPG that is bereft of companions.

My first essay, "Making Gods: The Nature and Media of Divinity in Apotheosis and Theosis", considers the question of apotheosis in ancient Rome and in *The Elder Scrolls* before considering the Christian doctrine of Theosis.

Jacob Torbeck's "Death and the Life After: Eschatology in *The Elder Scrolls V: Skyrim*", considers the eschatological elements of the world of *The Elder Scrolls*.

Michael Zeigler's first essay, "Dividing by Zero: Atheism and Apologia," considers the conflict between the Chimer and the Dwemer in the history of *Morrowind*, in the light of the contemporary conflict of Christianity with the New Atheism.

His second essay, "The Heart of the World: How Creation Stories Define Our Relationship to the Divine", considers creation stories and identity in our world and in the world of *The Elder Scrolls*.

Mark Hayse's essay "Procedural Theology in The Elder Scrolls Series" considers the mechanisms of *The Elder Scrolls* games in the context of a technological background of military history.

Closing the book, my essay "Ontological Frameworks: A New Technological Vocabulary for Doctrine," considers the many ramifications we, as theological thinkers, may derive from the fact that worlds like that which we encounter in *The Elder Scrolls* may exist in sustained realities outside of our minds.

Breadth and Audience

The games of *The Elder Scrolls* series are not equally represented here. As far as I can tell, only my essay mentions Redguard. None mention the mobile games with more than a passing comment. The most mentioned are *Morrowind* and *Skyrim*, followed *Oblivion*. This makes some great sense as *Morrowind* is hailed by many as their introduction to the series and one of the truly great RPG experiences of their lives. I am among these. And *Skyrim*, like *Morrowind*, deals with themes of divinity, prophecy and the larger mythological landscape of the world of *The Elder Scrolls.*

In a slowly growing corpus of works by academic theologians in the field of video games, we hope that this book can function in a few different ways. First, for those who are simply curious about where and how theology engages this excellent series of games, we hope that the work here will be an invitation to think more deeply. For those who perhaps consider video games to be a shallow or foolish form of entertainment, we also submit our considerations as theologians and religious scholars.

But perhaps our largest audience is other theological thinkers who wish to engage with this new medium, or any of the other media of popular culture. This is a young field in our modern society (though not young as far as the Church is concerned, as a brief look at the Cappadocian Fathers' literary works will attest). Theological criticism of video games is in its infancy. We hope this book will be a step toward real discussion about games, not just as a concept, but in their concrete realities. If this work helps to establish a base of texts that may be used in classrooms to discuss video games as a proper object of theological reflection, then we have done our job.

There is, of course, one more reason we have written this book. We have seen something in these games, and in gaming in general, that speaks to us. We hear a voice calling us to use our imaginations, to exercise that divine faculty and to enjoy the fruits of others' labors. This book is also for those who have excited our imaginations, the creators of *The Elder Scrolls* series, from authors to 3D modelers to coders, project managers and PR folks. Finally, of course, it is for that One great Creator who has worked out in our world a divine theme of joy which many of us have heard notes of in our playing of these games.

To that One, all we do is submitted for correction and resurrection.

Joshua Wise

Silver Spring, MD 2014

Endnotes

1 See Danielle Elizabeth Tumminio, *God and Harry Potter at Yale: Teaching Faith and Fantasy Fiction In An Ivy League Classroom*, (Unlocking Press, 2010).

Trinity and Tribunal

By Joshua Gonnerman

Introduction

As sub-creators and readers of texts,[1] we always draw on what we know. The conceptual material from which we create and read serves a vital role, both to provide content for our creations, and to provide a framework for understanding what we read. The Western world is no longer Christian (if it ever was), but it is undeniably post-Christian. The themes and images of Christian belief hover, if not as truths, at least as ghosts in the background of every mind which is embedded in the Western tradition with any depth. Countless young minds and mouths were trained to profess those central points of Christian doctrine which are encapsulated in the Creeds. Flannery O'Connor once wrote that "while the South is hardly Christ-centered, it is most certainly Christ-haunted. The Southerner, who isn't convinced of it, is very much afraid that he may have been formed in the image and likeness of God."[2] The Christ who haunts the South in O'Connor's essay is a foreboding specter, suggesting the possibility of worlds we had not accounted for and warning us that we may be on the wrong path. In our day, ghosts are weaker than they once were and we no longer fear them. Yet they remain, not as figures which strike fear in our hearts, but as echoes of memory, as a part of the conceptual backdrop against which our thoughts are patterned and from which they draw their material. The articles of faith have continued to exercise a certain authority over our imaginations and, only at the present moment have we reached the point where it seems they may drop out entirely from the minds of the average John and Jane on the street.

But the notion of the Trinity is not only an article of faith; it is also a "mystery." There are many notions in the Christian tradition which are regularly and profoundly misunderstood. Incarnation, Church, Eucharist, Trinity: all of these involve some sort of cognitive tension. God, but human. Institutional, but charismatic. Bread, but flesh. Three, but one. All of these ideas tend to fall prey to the one idea of "mystery."

Kierkegaard tells us: "This, then, is the ultimate paradox of thought: to want to discover something that itself cannot think."[3] We find here that which cannot be thought, and the attempt to discover it. A robust understanding of "mystery" does not see it as something which we cannot understand, and thus should not try; it is, rather, a bottomless well from which we may draw, an endless mine where we can always find riches, if we will but look. When "mystery" transcends human reason, this is no excuse not to deploy reason; rather, it is a promise that the meaning of the mystery is inexhaustible, always rewarding. The Christian story is, at its heart, an embracing of that attempt. We begin with the idea of Christ; as developed and defined, we learn from Nicaea that Christ is eternally begotten, in rejection of other perspectives. The Arian claim that "there was when he was not" is relegated to the outer darkness and thus, for all time, Christians are bound to the belief that Christ is fully, truly and unequivocally God. But how can we understand the idea that Christ is God? Does this mean that there is more than one God? Far be it from us to admit such a notion!

As strange, as wondrous, as incredible as it may seem, we come to the declaration that Christ is God; yet, Christ is not the same as the eternal source of his begetting. He is begotten of the Father and he mediates the Spirit. To take seriously the identity categories of the ancient tradition, we must maintain that these are distinct identities, not different masks worn by the one same God; yet all are equally and truly the one God. The liturgical Preface of the Holy Trinity, addressing the Father, says: "Who with your only-begotten Son and the Holy Spirit, are one God, one Lord: not in the singularity of one person, but in the Trinity of one substance. For what, through your revelation, we believe about your glory, we likewise hold about your Son and about the Holy Spirit, without difference of distinction. That in the confession of true and everlasting Godhead, alike the particularity of persons, and alike the unity of essence, and alike the equality of majesty may be adored."[4] This resonant formula highlights the importance of holding in tension both dimensions of the trinitarian paradox. When it is sung in the Latin, the very chant follows the same pattern for *proprietas* and *unitas*, thus performing the balance which faith finds between oneness and threeness in the Godhead. Without this emphasis, the mystery is lost, the paradox is broken. Likewise, the "equality of majesty" speaks to the orthodox rejection of the sort of hierarchy among the divine Persons which makes one to be greater and one lesser. The Father is the source of the other two Persons, but their shared divinity must lead us to profess that they share the selfsame glory.

It would be strange to expect all the complexities of the doctrine of the Trinity to seep into the cultural imagination, to be used by the sub-creators of other worlds and systems. Nevertheless, certain "vestiges of the Trinity" (to misappropriate Augustine's phrase) do manage to insinuate themselves here and there. In the world of video games, one might point to three goddesses and the Triforce in *The Legend of Zelda: Ocarina of Time.*

Sometimes, however, the doctrine of the Trinity is a clear point of reference for sub-creators, and they model their sub-creation, to a greater or lesser extent, on this idea received from Christian tradition. The religious beliefs and expressions of the Dunmer in *Morrowind* are a clear example of this. The two main idioms of Dunmer religion are the Nerevarine cult of the wild Ashlanders and the Tribunal Temple of the city Dunmer. Each of these presents a clear analogue to one of the central doctrines of Christianity; the Nerevarine prophecies contain resonances of Christ as the Messiah, while the religion of the Temple finds its inspiration in the doctrine of the Trinity and the church structures more commonly associated with Christianity, especially with Catholicism. In this volume, Thaddeus Winker and Matthew Franks both addresss the Nerevarine messianism, while I offer reflections on the Trinitarian roots of the Tribunal and the churchly roots of its Temple.

Tribunal and Trinity

At first glance, the Trinitarian inspiration of the Tribunal is quite clear. We encounter the worship of three deities, Vivec, Almalexia and Sotha Sil, under a unified identity of "the Tribunal." Even the name seems chosen to evoke "Trinity." Their alternate name of "Almsivi" shows a deep interconnection between the three, for from the three names, *Alma*lexia, Sotha *Sil*, and *Vi*vec, one name has been forged. Yet, the more closely we examine the Tribunal, the more evident it becomes that the similarities are superficial.

All modes of acting and interacting arise from given contexts. This is no less true if the object of interaction is the realm of the supernatural. Any sub-creative effort worth its salt will stand, at least in the mind of the sub-creator, against a backdrop from which it has arisen. The great exemplar (and particularly germane to theme of sub-creation) is that of J. R. R. Tolkien's *The Lord of the Rings*. The world of Middle-earth had been gestating and developing in Tolkien's mind since World War I, when he began to write about Beren and Lúthien, as a way of expressing his love for his future wife, Edith, from whom he was separated. It expanded to the capacious mythology which we find in *The Silmarillion*, with the *History of Middle-earth* volumes, at times showing earlier forms of it and, at times, fleshing out what we find in *The Silmarillion*. It is against this backdrop that Tolkien conceived *The Lord of the Rings* and it is this backdrop which lent such richness and mythological depth to his famous book.

No mean feat of sub-creation went into the construction of Tamriel and *The Elder Scrolls* games can stand next to Tolkien's works as a worthy example of the sub-creative endeavor. It is, then, no surprise that we will find an "historical" background to the subjects which we are investigating here.

The ancient religion of the Dunmer was one of ancestor worship. Those who went before them remained present as agents in their world: their wrath could be incurred, their favor could be curried, their activity could be prompted. Sacred rites bound them visibly to the world, so that their presence was deeply tangible. The exceptionally deep reverence which the Dunmer had for their ancestors led to a particularly strict ban on (non-sanctioned) necromantic practices.[5] Related to the ancestors were the Aedra, primeval spirits who were significant in the creation of the world; the Dunmer regarded the Aedra, therefore, as being, in some sense, their originators. In the language of the primeval elves, the Aldmer, the word "Aedra" meant "our ancestors."[6] As ancestral spirits, the Aedra were seen as signs of permanence and of stability.

The other agents which the Dunmer of old worshipped were the Daedra, those who were "not the ancestors." Where the ancestral quality of the Aedra gave them connotations of order and connection to Dunmer culture, the Daedra were deeply alien forces and tended to represent change. They were feared by the mortal races and most religious authorities sought to stomp out their worship; however, the cult of the Daedra thrived among the ancient Dunmer.

From time to time, great heroes arose among the peoples of Nerevar. For our discussion of the Tribunal, we must pay attention to a certain group of heroes: Nerevar, Vivec, Almalexia, Sotha Sil and Voryn Dagoth. As any student of history knows, there are often conflicting accounts from which we must draw a narrative. What follows below is one such narrative, with attention given where it seems appropriate to divergent evidence.

The ancient Dwemer were a highly advanced race and created mechanical cities to house them, mechanical servants to tend to their needs, mechanical *animiculi* to guard them. They lived underground, distant from the other races, and came to scorn their ways. As an account attributed to Vivec says, they "scorned the Daedra, and mocked our foolish rituals, and preferred instead their gods of Reason and Logic."[7] The Dwemer were united with the Chimer (the forebears of the Dunmer) in 1E 401, in an effort to thrust out Nordic invaders. Dumac of the Dwemer and Nerevar of the Chimer ruled the nation of Resdayn (in modern Morrowind) jointly. But there were always tensions, often rooted in the religion of the Chimer and the irreligion of Dwemer. The greatest architect of the Dwemer, Kagrenac, obtained the Heart of Lorkhan (the trickster-deity who led the Aedra to create the world) and planned to use its power to forge a being to be called Numidium, a mechanical god.

When Voryn Dagoth (the leader of House Dagoth) learned of this, he informed Nerevar; Nerevar was outraged, regarding it as an act of blasphemy for mortals to create a god. A growing sense of mistrust led to war between the Chimer and the Dwemer. In 1E 700, this war culminated at Red Mountain, then the capital of the Dwemer. Nerevar and Dumac faced off against each other, and both fell from terrible wounds. In desperation, Kagrenac turned his tools on the Heart and he disappeared with all the Dwemer.[8] Those tools were taken by Voryn Dagoth. The wounded Nerevar went to consult with the Tribunal[9] about what to do with them; the Tribunal counseled that they be studied to unlock their secrets. Nerevar agreed, on the condition that an oath to the Daedra Azura be sworn against using them to make gods. This oath was kept for a time, but eventually was broken and Azura cursed them in its breaking.[10] Sotha Sil, whom BRM presents as the main force behind the use of the tools of Kagrenac, accused Azura and the old gods in general of being capricious. "We are the new gods, born of the flesh, and wise and caring of the needs of our people. Spare us your threats and chiding, inconstant spirit. We are bold and fresh, and will not fear you."[11] Azura's curse manifested in the darkening of the Chimer skin and the reddening of their eyes and she left them with the warning that they were blind in the darkness.[12] The Tribunal erected the Ghostfence to keep Voryn Dagoth/Dagoth Ur in the Red Mountain.

The Dunmer no longer needed to cower before spirits, but could address their gods face to face. The Tribunal ruled over them for long ages, until eventually, the Nerevarine, rumored to be Nerevar reborn, came towards the end of the Third Era. He slew Almalexia (who had first slain Sotha Sil), and the dark Dagoth Ur, and Vivec disappeared. But the Tribunal had long been disconnected with Dunmer life and their worship seems to have continued, until the Red Mountain erupted in 4E 5, rendering much of the island of Vvardenfell uninhabitable.[13] The Dunmer then returned to their old ancestor worship and the gods of the Tribunal were demoted to being three saints among many.

This brief overview of the rise and fall of the Tribunal makes clear that the resonance between Tribunal and Trinity is largely external. The Christian theological tradition has located the distinction among the Persons of the Trinity in their relation to each other. At the root of the Western tradition of trinitarian theology, Augustine discusses a metaphysic-inflected grammar of the Trinity: "The chief point then that we must maintain is that whatever that supreme and divine majesty is called with reference to itself is said substance-wise; whatever it is called with reference to another is said not substance- but relationship-wise; and that such is the force of the expression 'of the same substance' in Father and Son and Holy Spirit, that whatever is said with reference to self about each of them is to be taken as adding up in all three to a singular and not to a plural."[14] As David Meconi puts it, this predication of relationship in the Trinity "demonstrates an unequaled type of being whose identity is completely constituted by personal relation."[15] While much of the depth of his *De Trinitate* was lost to later generations, this notion that the Persons were distinguished through relation remained a key element in Western theological thought.

In the East, the Cappadocian fathers were instrumental in the formation of a developed Trinitarian theology and further reflections have taken their development as a starting point. The first council of Nicaea, addressing the Arian controversy, provides the starting point for a dogmatic theology of the Trinity, especially in the words that would develop into the Niceno-Constantinipolitan creed. In 325, the council defined against the Arians that Christ was "God, of God; Light, of Light; Very God, of very God; Begotten, not made; Being of one substance with the

Father." The council of Nicaea, received as the first ecumenical council, functions in the Christian imagination as the definitive settlement of the disputed question. In fact, the battles were far from over and only seem to have been more or less settled at the first council of Constantinople. In that interim period, the Cappadocians took up a central role in the theological reception of the conciliar definition. Gregory of Nazianzus has been especially influential and it is for his "Theological Orations" on the Trinity that he has been given the name, "Gregory the Theologian", in the Eastern Churches. In these Orations, he, too, highlights relation as the key to understanding difference in the Trinity. He recounts how the heirs of Arian theology claimed that "Father" was a name of an essence or action, so that the Son cannot have the same essence, not being Unbegotten. Gregory rejects their options, preferring "a third, and truer possibility. My expert friends, it is this: 'Father' designates neither the substance nor the activity, but the relationship, the manner of being, which holds good between the Father and the Son. Just as with us these names indicate kindred and affinity, so here too they designate the sameness of stock, of parent and offspring."[16] Thus, it is through the relation that the Son has to the Father that we know the Son shares the same nature as the Father. He says similarly, when he asks how the Son differs from the Spirit: "It is their difference in, so to say, 'manifestation' or mutual relationship, which has caused the difference in names."[17]

While we need not adhere strictly enough to the old principle that "like begets like" to conflict with evolutionary theory, we may recognize a general reality to it, which makes it a useful tool in theological reflection. A human father has a certain sameness of nature with his progeny, but their natures remain numerically distinct. Martin Sheen is of the same kind as Charlie Sheen and Emilio Estevez, but their natures are not numerically one. In Aristotelian terminology, they share the same second substance (that is, they fall under the same substantial category of "human being," and Emilio and Charlie do so because they were begotten by human parents), but they do not share the same first substance (that is, they are not the same individual), and thus, they do not have a numerical identity of essence. In the Godhead, we cannot permit such a sharp distinction between the persons, or else honesty would demand that we emend our creed to say, "I believe in three Gods." Thus, we find one numerical identity of essence in the Persons of the Trinity. In God, there is no abstraction or universal distinguished from a particularity. There is simply (with a "simplicity" so complete, we encounter it as infinitely multivalent) the Divine Essence in which the Three Hypostases subsist. Thus, the Trinitarian theology of the Cappadocians has found its classical (though perhaps over-simplistic) formulation: "One ousia, three hypostases." The formulation he gives in letter 101 gave rise to the famous *alius et alius, non aliud et aliud*; after saying that the Savior is constituted by different "things" (*allo kai allo*), but not different persons (*ouk allos kai allos*) he goes on to write: "I say different things (*allo kai allo*) meaning the reverse of what is the case in the Trinity. There we have "others" (*allos kai allos*) in order not to confuse the subjects or hypostases, but not other *things* (*ouk allo kai allo*): the three are one and the same thing *qua* Godhead."[18]

This radical unity is a far cry from the members of the Tribunal. The unity we find there is makeshift and external, as is their very divinity.[19] The Persons of the Trinity are defined by their relations to each other. The members of the Tribunal, on the other hand, are defined by their relation to that which is outside, to Nerevar, for it is he who brought together a queen and two generals as a ruling structure.[20] Because their identity as Tribunal is derived from an outside source, they are substantially distinct, and one member of the Tribunal can act or be encountered without the other two, whereas the unity of action and intimacy of union of the three Persons of the Trinity is a given in classical trinitarian theology. This autonomy of action under an assumed and deceptive unity of identity creates a jarring dissonance between the mode of presentation in the Tribunal and their realities. The tension of this dissonance cannot be maintained and in the end, they turn on each other, Almalexia demanding the death of Sotha Sil. Because their deity derives from an outside source, it is imperfect and they can be destroyed. Both of these are enacted at the end, when Almalexia performs autonomy of action in directly moving against Sotha Sil. The false unity created by the single name "Almsivi" cannot hold and the tension created by this pretense leads to the demonstration, not only of the possibility of death, but of its fated necessity for the false gods, as no effort on the part of the player character can keep Sotha Sil from destruction (wrought, pace the Reclamations, by Almalexia, not the Nerevarine). The introduction of death into the Trinity in the person of Jesus Christ was the subversion of expectation, the striking out into new territory, to redeem those who are lost there. In the case of the Tribunal, death was the inevitable result of an attempt to subsume autonomous entities under a single identity.

The Tribunal, in the end, lacks the substantial unity which is the distinctive of the Trinity. It is not a trinity, but a tritheistic system, masquerading as a singular "Almsivi." The focus on internal relation which lends the Trinity internal coherence is utterly absent in the Tribunal, and its dissolution into discord was inevitable. At the same time, it is a modeling after the great mystery of the Godhead. The analogies between the Temple and Christian hierarchies (most notably the Archcanon as a clear analogue to the bishop of Rome) make this Trinitarian influence all the clearer. By tinging the Tribunal with hints of treachery, and the Tribunal in the breaking of the oath Nerevar had them swear to Azura, and in the possibility that they even murdered their master, and in the hint of conspiracy around the Temple's maintenance of open writings and secret writings which preserve strikingly different accounts of the events at Red Mountain, there is (whether consciously or not) an implicit discrediting of the Christian religion and the Church which holds to it. The fact that these questions are connected with the death of Nerevar renders the implicit indictment even more nefarious.

But the analogy, while clear, remains distant, and it seems unlikely that the *j'accuse* is an intentional effort to undermine Christian faith. It is even less that any believing Christian will have her faith seriously shaken by the secrets of the Tribunal. In the end, the main function of the whole is the preservation of a Christ-haunted landscape in the West. For this echo of our faith in modern pop culture, as we are directed by the Doxology, let us "praise Father, Son and Holy Ghost!"

WORKS CITED:

St. Augustine of Hippo. *The Trinity.* Translated by Edmund Hill. Works of St. Augustine: A Translation for the 21st Century. Hyde Park: New City Press, 1991.

St. Gregory of Nazianzus. *On God and Christ: The Five Theological Orations and Two Letters to Cledonius.* Edited by John Behr. Popular Patristics Series. Crestwood, NY: St. Vladimir's Seminary Press, 2002. 84.

Kierkegaard, Søren. *Philosophical Fragments and Johannes Climacus.* Translated by Howard and Edna Hong. Princeton: *Princeton* University Press, 1985.

Meconi, David Vincent. *The One Christ: Augustine's Doctrine of Deification.* Washington, DC: The Catholic University of America Press, 2013.

O' Connor, Flannery. *Mystery and Manners: Occasional Prose.* Edited by Sally and Robert Fitzgerald. New York: Farrar, Straus and Giroux, 1969.

In-game books consulted through the Unofficial Elder Scrolls Pages, at http://www.uesp.net/wiki/Main_Page

Endnotes

[1] I use "text" in the sense given it by literary theory, where it means any artistic object which we are able to "read" for meaning.

[2] Flannery O'Connor, "Some Aspects of the Grotesque in Southern Fiction," in *Mystery and Manners: Occasional Prose*, ed. Sally and Robert Fitzgerald (New York: Farrar, Straus and Giroux, 1969), 44-45.

[3] Søren Kierkegaard, *Philosophical Fragments and Johannes Climacus*, trans. Howard and Edna Hong (Princeton: Princeton University Press, 1985), 37.

[4] *qui cum unigenito filio tuo et spiritu sancto unus es deus, unus es dominus; non in unius singularitate personae, sed in unius trinitate substantiae. Quod enim de tua gloria, revelante te, credimus, hoc de filio tuo, hoc de spiritu sancto, sine differentia discretionis sentimus. Ut in confessione verae sempiternaeque deitatis, et in personis proprietas, et in essentia unitas, et in majestate adoretur aequalitas.*

[5] Forms of ancestor worship existed among many of the peoples of Tamriel, but they were not so pronounced as among the Dunmer.

[6] *Aedra and Daedra.* Where references list only a title, they refer to books found in the Elder Scrolls games, usually in *Morrowind.*

[7] *The Battle of Red Mountain and the Rise and Fall of the Tribunal* (henceforth *BRM*). *BRM* is purportedly an account of the central events which lay behind the Tribunal's rise to power, recounted to a dissident priest under interrogation. There are two significant caveats with which we must approach this text. 1) It may not actually be derived from Vivec; the claim of its origin could easily be fabricated to lend it credibility. 2) If it is from Vivec, the antiquity of the events is an obstacle (as the text itself says, "Who can clearly recall the events of the distant past"). 3) Granted authenticity and memory, we must still beware, as the purported origin places it in a decidedly biased context, which may lead us to take it with a grain of salt. That said, the authenticity of the text is suggested by the substantive account it gives of these events, unparalleled in other known texts. A concern for bias is somewhat assuaged, as Vivec does not emerge in a positive light (though other accounts paint him worse); still, the dissidence of the priest who transmitted it could account for this. The question of memory remains a concern; still, the intriguing character of the text leads me to favor it.

[8] We find an alternate tradition in *Nerevar at Red Mountain* (*NRM*), a secret compilation of Ashlander traditions kept by the Temple among the apographa; it claims that Voryn Dagoth/ Dagoth Ur murdered Kagrenac. It further claims that Nerevar summoned Azura when the tools were brought to him, and that she showed him how to use them to destroy the Dwemer.

[9] His queen, Almalexia, and his generals, Sotha Sil and Vivec.

[10] *NRM* claims that the Tribunal murdered Nerevar with a poisoned ritual, and that it was for this murder, more than for the foresworn oath, that Azura punished them. Nerevar has dropped out of the narrative in *BRM*; Azura warns the Tribunal that he will return to punish them, but he is not present when the oath is broken. A reader might extrapolate from the narrative of *BRM* that Nerevar died from his wounds; nevertheless, the silence about his death is notable. For another version of Nerevar's death, see Matthew Frank's essay in this volume.

[11] *BRM.*

[12] In keeping with its claim that the Tribunal murdered Nerevar, *NRM* has Azura interpreting the Dunmer appearance as "like ghouls" who had devoured their king.

[13] *The Reclamations: The Fall of the Tribunal and the Rise of the New Temple.*

[14] Augustine, *The Trinity* 5.8.9, trans. Edmund Hill (Hyde Park: New City Press, 1991), 195.

[15] David Vincent Meconi, SJ, *The One Christ: Augustine's Doctrine of Deification.* (Washington, DC: The Catholic University of America Press, 2013), 5.

[16] Gregory of Nazianzus, oration 29.16, in *On God and Christ: The Five Theological Orations and Two Letters to Cledonius*, ed. John Behr (Crestwood, NY: St. Vladimir's Seminary Press, 2002), 84.

[17] Gregory of Nazianzus, oration 31.9, in *On God and Christ*, 123.

[18] Gregory of Nazianzus, letter 101.5, in *On God and Christ*, 157.

[19] It is common to worry that the "essence" not lead to an unwitting admittance of a fourth to the Trinity, from which the other three arise. One could take the Tools of Kagrenac as an extreme "quaternitizing" of the Trinity. They are the source of the divinity of the Tribunal, and thus, of their (loosely) unified identity; a divine Tribunal has far greater cohesion than an elvish one. If we must avoid falling into thought patterns which permit the unconscious reckoning of essence or ousia as a fourth which sources the three, the Tools render explicit what those thought patterns look like. For a discussion of divinity in relation to the Tribunal, see Joshua Wise's essay on apotheosis in this volume.

[20] This is further problematized by the ambiguous nature of the relationship the members of the Tribunal hold towards Nerevar. The suggestions of betrayal in the hidden writings of the Temple render their unity, not only externally imposed, but utterly counterfeit, by maliciously destroying its source.

As I Lay Dying:
Witness and Death in Morrowind[1]

BY MATTHEW FRANKS

In a sunken shipwreck somewhere along the southern coast of Vvardenfell, amid the island-littered sea east of Vivec, the prophesied Nerevarine perished, drowned without witness but for few fish of the deep.

The scene described above is one of the more profound experiences offered by a video role-playing game and exactly what makes it profound is the subject of the following essay. Whether or not video games constitute a new form of art is not part our argument here – the fact is that some video game experiences, such as that found in *The Elder Scrolls III: Morrowind*, are sufficiently interesting to warrant some deliberate reflection. In so doing we will follow along certain lines of artistic reflection, as one of the characteristics of role-playing games is that there is a narrative arc[2] that is important to the experience of the game play.

What makes the experience described above – that of an igno-minious and unwitnessed death within a narrative arc that is supposed to conclude with a glorious and celebrated messianic fulfillment – is that such experiences are rare, whether in literature or video gaming. They are perhaps impossible in prose – while characters within a novel can cer-tainly perish, the dominant voice (that of the author) cannot, or it would be the end of the book, and likely a very unsatisfying one. It is possible for a character to speak after death (as Addie does in Faulkner's *As I Lay Dying*), but in such cases the death itself is subsumed within the larger narrative structure, which is able to speak from an imaginative perspec-tive outside of death. In a first-person video game such as *Morrowind*, the death of the player's character is the end of the game.[3] Of course the game can be restarted from the beginning or (much more conveniently and commonly) from a previously saved position. But the point is that the virtual death signals an ending – restarting the game or replaying it from a previous point is the insistence that things should not have ended in such a way, and that whatever story concluding with a virtual death is unsatisfactory and should be essentially "rewritten." The open-ended game play of *Morrowind* also offers more opportunity for a solitary char-acter death than many other games; generally, characters perish at least in the company of the adversary that defeats them. While individual per-ceptions differ, it certainly can be argued that *Morrowind* has something of a "lonely"[4] feeling about it; there is no "adventuring party" as in most third-person[5] computer role-playing games. A character's death (even if it is the main character) is often not the end of the game; other mem-bers might be able to affect the situation. Even if this is not the case, the character's death takes place in the company of others and so is viewed in what might be called a social context, rather than an individual one. Death in *Morrowind*, however, is an individual experience.

The point is that we will begin our examination from the experience of loss in *Morrowind*, rather than the experience of fulfillment. *Morrowind* provides very fertile ground here, as the game experience is both very personal for reasons we have touched on above, and the narrative arc is essentially messianic. The heroic narrative arc is, of course, not rare in video gaming and in video role-playing games it is almost taken for granted; messianism is somewhat less common. *Morrowind's* messianism is especially pointed; the world of *Morrowind* is sufficiently unlike our mundane reality to put distance between direct comparisons, but the Nerevarine as savior of an outcaste race under the political control of a powerful world-empire and champion of a religious movement that is related to, but overturns, the prevailing faith system is a little on the nose. While the fulfillment of the messianic story arc is the primary goal in the game, the open-ended structure of the game play allows many events that are not directly tied to this goal to affect the player. Allowing the player the choice to take up the messianic role or not provides a certain ambiguity to the "purpose" of the player's character in the game and it is this ambiguity, combined with the intensely individual experience of the game, that creates the pervasively existential tone of *Morrowind*.

Morrowind is an existential video game *par excellence*. Both the groundbreaking technical innovations and the traditional role-playing game devices employed in the third installment of *The Elder Scrolls* work to create a virtual reality that is saturated with the sense of "having been thrown" into the world. Much of the drama of the game is formed by the construction of a sense of meaning and place in the world for the individual character. The "unformed" nature of the character is, of course, combined with the predetermined fate of that character as dictated by *Morrowind's* story arc – to fulfill the messianic role necessary to complete the game. The artistic conceit of the game is that the player does not necessarily know (or at least know for certain) that it is his character that is to become the messianic savior of Vvardenfell. The game begins with a prophecy of the Nerevarine that applies to the character is some respects, but exactly how, or if, it will be fulfilled is not certain. Experienced gamers, of course, assume that their character is to become the Nerevarine and they are correct in their assumption; very few games remove the character from the ultimate concern of the story, though there are certain exceptions, as we will discuss later.

The existential themes of *Morrowind* are found in different aspects of the game. Some are present in the events that occur in the narrative arc and, as such, can be discussed as one might examine similar themes found in a novel. However, many existential elements present themselves in the system of the game itself and in the context of video gaming, in general. To better draw out the important elements, we must look at *Morrowind*, both as an imaginative experience in its own right and as a game in the context of other games. Themes such as character formation, role within a messianic story arc and the perspective of witness can be better explored by comparing *Morrowind* with other exceptional games that touch upon those themes, such as *Ultima IV, Below the Root* and *Ace Combat 4*.

But we must first address what we mean by "existentialism." The term is loosely used and difficult to define, even in the context of philosophy as a discipline, but we can start with the fact that existentialism focuses on "the uniqueness of each human individual as distinguished from abstract universal human qualities."[6] *The Cambridge Dictionary of Philosophy* (as any other source material on existentialism would do) goes on to note the historical origins of existentialism in Christian thinkers such as Pascal, and Kierkegaard. One might press the issue and connect existentialism with the Christian monastic movement, which emphasizes the individual experience in the light of the divine over the communal experience. Existentialism need not necessarily be connected with theism; indeed, many existentialists take as a fact of existence the absence of a divinity. But as theology is the unifying theme of the essay series of which this is a part, we will look at existentialism primarily in this context and *Morrowind's* messianic elements obviously lend themselves to this kind of examination.

Whether Heidegger ought to be considered an existentialist is debated, but many of his themes are existentialist ones: "existential categories and ideas such as anxiety in the presence of death, our sense of being 'thrown' into existence, and our temptation to choose anonymity over authenticity in our conduct."[7] The aforementioned categories will serve very well for a discussion of existentialism in the context of video games, in general, and *Morrowind*, in particular.

While the heroic/messianic identity of the player's character in *Morrowind* is fairly conventional, what *Morrowind* excels at is the creation of an "existential mood." Let us take up Heidegger's concept of *geworfenheit*, that sense of "being thrown" into the world. Heidegger is certainly not the only thinker to touch upon it; Voegelin, perhaps refining Shakespeare's reflection that "all the world's a stage, and all the men and women merely players," (*As You Like It*, II.vii.139-140) likens the human experience to that of a player committed to a drama without knowing exactly what his role is to be.[8]

In *Morrowind's* opening sequence, the player's character comes into consciousness on the prison boat putting into port at Seyda Neen; one of the first (if not the very first) opportunities for player action is to input a name when asked about his identity. Being asked one's name elegantly points out the core existential question – who am I? *Morrowind* deftly incorporates the construction of the player's virtual persona – the identity of the player within the bounds of the game-world – into a series of familiar encounters, whether with concerned fellow travelers or the bureaucrat processing a file. This is substantially different from the early game experiences of "rolling up" characters in an adventuring party[9] found in many fantasy role-playing games, from *The Bard's Tale* to *Wizardry* to *Might and Magic*.[10] The process of self-questioning (Who am I? When was I born? Where am I from?) creates a significant level of identification between the player and his virtual presence in the game and places great emphasis on the question of identity in the narrative.

Simply playing the game from a first -person perspective, as opposed to controlling an "adventuring party," puts the player in a solitary frame of mind. Forming a character in *Morrowind* asks the player to envision how he sees himself acting as an individual in the game world. Will he take a confrontational, combative stance; a stealthy, nuanced persona, etc. This choice affects the player's character engagement with the virtual environment as an individual; by contrast, character creation in adventuring party role-playing games is dominated by strategizing about "party balance" – creating characters of differing skills that complement each other and work well as a team.

One element of the compelling character creation sequence[11] in *Morrowind,* the answering of moral dilemmas to determine one's class within the game, seems an obvious nod to character creation found in the classic video role-playing game *Ultima IV*. Despite the limitations of early computing, *Ultima IV's* beginning narrative draws the player deftly into the game world and forms his character from a series of ethical dilemmas asked by a gypsy fortuneteller. *Ultima IV* was groundbreaking on many levels, but with its top-down (third person) perspective and the accumulation of the standard "adventuring party" for game play, it could not take the existential mood to the extreme that is found in *Morrowind*.

This is not to argue that *Morrowind* is necessarily superior to *Ultima IV*, *The Bard's Tale*, *Baldur's Gate* or other adventuring party games, only that the sense of the existential is heightened in *Morrowind* due to its mode of character creation and its first-person perspective. Indeed, one of the curious effects of playing *Morrowind* is a profound sense of solitude, whereas with the adventure party games one often gets a sense of "virtual comradery." The death of an individual character in such games is something of a communal event – the player might be concerned about how the death of one character will affect the performance of the remaining party, which party member might be able to resurrect or replace the lost member, whether it is worth restarting the game to erase the unfortunate occurrence and whether it may be in fact an opportune moment to find out if the party would be better off replacing the fallen member. While players might experience a certain attachment to individual characters, it is really the overall success of the adventuring party that is of interest to the player – in this way, the player's identification with the characters is more distant and abstract.

The first-person perspective creates an existential mood in the same way that first-person narratives tend to encourage readers to identify with characters – the obvious difference being that in a written narrative, the reader cannot control the actions of the protagonist and, instead, must embark on the narrative journey as witness rather than participant. In terms of the narrative, the witnesses in video games, such as they are, are the non-player characters controlled by the computer. Given this, it is surprising to what extent their reactions affect the choices of the player in *Morrowind*. Stealing from or harming non-player characters causes them to react negatively to the player's character, if those actions are witnessed. If not, however, such acts do not affect non-player perceptions. It is possible for the player's character to have a "heroic" public persona (and even fulfill his destiny as Nerevarine), and yet commit acts considered socially unacceptable.

The ability within the game to have a split between a public and private persona is very important to the existential feel of *Morrowind*. It simulates the dual response to the existential question of "Who am I?" that we engage in our own lived experience. "Who am I?" in regards to myself and when no one is watching, and "Who am I?" in terms of how others perceive me. One could argue that there is also the question of "Who am I?" in terms of fate, destiny or the metaphysical sense due to the narrative arc that is larger than present *Morrowind* society itself (having to do with the past, the future, cosmology, etc.). This would be the existential question framed in terms of the individual's confrontation with the divine – "Who am I?" in a lasting, ultimate sense – what role do I have in the story that truly matters.

The possible difference between a private persona and public perception, of course, brings to mind that perennial ethical question posed by Thrasymachus/Glaucon – Is it better to be truly just, or simply to appear to be just?[12] The game itself probably leans more towards being truly just or, at least, generally observant of the basic ethics of society; it is generally easier to make one's way in Vvardenfell if one is socially acceptable in terms of game play and there is little that cannot be obtained in the game by legitimate means, while breaking the conventions of *Morrowind* carries substantial risks.

One could argue, however, that being able to restart/reload a game whenever one is witnessed acting badly effectively removes even the virtual penalty of unethical behavior. A character could quite easily fulfill the Thrasymachus/Glaucon ideal of appearing perfectly just in *Morrowind* society, while reaping all the benefits of acting badly. Some players, of course, might find it interesting to live notoriously, accepting the difficulties caused by breaking social conventions, especially when they have amassed enough power to be able to largely flaunt those difficulties.

But the player cannot decide to be the Nerevarine; the virtual others of *Morrowind* must decide that he is their prophesied messiah. In this sense, the conclusion of the narrative arc rests outside the player's whim – while having a great deal of freedom in game terms to do what he wishes, the character must indeed act in certain ways if he is to complete the game.[13]

One expects that players will generally bring their own moral sensibilities into game play, especially if they are able to identify with the character or are involved in the creation of the character. In such cases, the character is a representation of one's persona and his conduct would tend to mirror the player's. But in regards to the witness of the character's acts, the removal of any real social consequence would be somewhat different. Again, there would be a difference here between *Morrowind* and MMOs, where virtual social consequences can bleed more easily into what one perceives as real social consequences, as many members of the game's society are connected to real people, rather than run by machines.

The element of a character's fated messiahship also marks a distinction between *Morrowind* and MMOs; the singular nature of a messiah means that MMOs must steer clear of such elements – if all players could be messiahs, none of them would be.

In light of the concept of "witness," we might contrast the messianic identity of the character to the existential "temptation to choose anonymity over authenticity in our conduct." There is certainly no doubt, that in mundane life, one often seeks out anonymity – there is the very understandable desire to fit well into society and a perfectly socialized life would entail anonymity for all but the most exceptional individuals.[14] Video games, due to the active nature of the form, perhaps alleviate the tension of forgoing authenticity[15] for anonymity. Almost all video games cast the player in the role of hero or savior in some way and role-playing games tend to do this quite explicitly. As we have seen, in *Morrowind*, the "true" (or for our purpose, the "authentic") role of the player's character, from the perspective of narrative arc of the game, is to become the Nerevarine. Interestingly, the game allows the option, however, of forgoing this and sinking into anonymity...or infamy. A quick review of posts regarding what their characters do in *Morrowind* reveals that many hardly mention finishing the game at all, instead focusing on what virtual homes they have taken over, how they procure rare items and large amount of money or how they terrorize inhabitants.[16]

We could attribute this to the fact that *Morrowind* offers a great deal outside the main narrative to keep the player busy; the completion of the narrative (especially since this must be accomplished in a certain manner) offers less variety than the less restricted array of actions, appearances, reactions of non-player characters, etc. that are available to players. "Winning" the game requires a set of defined actions and so there is comparatively less to discuss than the endless permutations of existence within *Morrowind* – the "life" of the character, as it were.

Games, to reach a conclusion, generally require a winner (and loser); the drama of most sporting games is in the discovery of the identity of who will win, not whether someone will win. A video game with one player generally requires that player to be able to win.[17] With video role-playing games that have a narrative structure, the assumption is generally that the player is to be the hero or savior within the dramatic arc and so a major element of identity is already present at the beginning of the game. The role of the player's character is that of the winner, the savior, the hero. *Morrowind* is no exception in this regard, but I am aware of two interesting examples that alter the player's expectation of being the ultimate hero. *Below the Root* was a beautifully executed game based on the *Green Sky Trilogy* books by Zilpha Keatley

Snyder. Like *Morrowind*, the theme of messianism runs through *Below the Root*; the religious and social life of Green Sky hangs in the balance. But instead of becoming Green Sky's savior, the player is cast in the role of the one who rescues the savior, a refreshingly diminutive identity in a game that is all the more impressive for its overall sense of modesty.[18]

Perhaps in keeping with the "smallness" of the game, death does not enter into *Below the Root*; the character at worst can be imprisoned or knocked out, at which time he is returned to his home to take up the quest again. There is no sense of finality that would require the story to be "rewritten" (restarted). But anxiety in the face of death is perhaps the core existential dilemma, in the shadow of which all other questions of origin and identity find their ultimate meaning.

To return to the scene at the beginning of this essay, death in *Morrowind* can be an especially lonely experience. It may take place without witnesses, leading to a reflection on what it is to perish unobserved by society. Because the character is supposed to be the messianic figure, it also leads one to reflect on what it is to fail to achieve one's "true" role in society. He cannot be the true Nerevarine because he has failed; thus, the narrative cannot be complete until the story is rewritten. At the same time, the open-ended game play of *Morrowind* allows a player to enjoy the game apart from the narrative, with an identity removed from his presumed messianic role; outside the context of the narrative, character deaths become meaningless erasures. Within the context of the narrative, the death of the character as prophesied messiah is intolerable – if he dies,[19] then obviously he cannot be the messiah. The only meaningful death is actually that of the adversary, Dagoth Ur, as this is necessary for the completion of the prophecy and, hence, to the messianic identity of the player's character.

In a different way from *Morrowind* and *Below the Root*, *Ace Combat 4* invites a very interesting reflection on the player's sense of identity, especially in terms of both witness and death. While quite action-oriented, *Ace Combat 4* includes an impressive narrative element. The player takes on the role of an air combat ace and as he completes missions there are beautifully rendered cut scenes telling the story of a boy whose parents are killed when a fighter plane is shot down by the great ace of the enemy forces the player is fighting. One expects that the story will come around to reveal how that boy grows up to become the player's character who exacts revenge by shooting down the enemy ace in a final showdown. But as the story progresses, this seems less and less likely, as we learn that the boy comes to know the enemy ace when his town is occupied; the enemy ace is revealed to be an honorable man who, while excellent in combat, takes no joy in killing or war.

The player's character does indeed have to shoot down the enemy ace, but the cut scene that follows is fascinating; the boy telling the story is mourning the death of the enemy ace, rather than celebrating the player character's accomplishment. In the end, the antagonist is much more the central figure of the narrative than the player's character, at least in emotional terms. The story the player has been hearing is a letter written by the boy in honor of the enemy ace. While the boy supports the player's character in the larger war, the boy is telling the story so that the player's character will know the quality of his adversary. Such "de-centering" of the player's character shifts him from an object of witness to the witness himself. In *Morrowind*, the prophecy makes the character the object of witness in the narrative, bearing the weight of social expectations. This is why dying, especially dying an unwitnessed death, is so jarring in *Morrowind* – there is no one, not even an adversary, to judge him not to be the Nerevarine. There is no one to judge at all and so there is no meaning to the characters demise.

REFERENCES

The Cambridge Dictionary of Philosophy, Second Edition, ed. Robert Audi. Cambridge: Cambridge University Press, 1999.

Voegelin, Eric. *Israel and Revelation.* Baton Rouge: Louisiana State University Press, 1991.

Writing and the Digital Generation: Essays on New Media Rhetoric, ed. Heather Urbanski. Jefferson, NC: McFarland & Co., 2010.

ONLINE REFERENCES

http://www.quartertothree.com/game-talk/showthread.php?71546-Morrowind-Ten-years-later-and-it-s-still-an-amazing-game, accessed June 28, 2013.

http://www.neoseeker.com/forums/5665/t504620-morrowinds-best-bases-houses/, accessed June 28, 2013.

http://elderscrolls.wikia.com

www.uesp.net

Endnotes

[1] One could argue that most video games, not just role-playing video games, are framed in some story or other, and that the "back story" of *Morrowind* is substantially more developed than many novels.

[2] This excludes the genre of games that have multiple players simultaneously taking on first-person perspectives, such as MMOs (massively multiplayer online games).

[3] This is mentioned casually on many *Morrowind* discussion boards, for example: "And finally two companions, because travelling through Morrowind can be lonely." http://www.quartertothree.com/game-talk/showthread.php?71546-Morrowind-Ten-years-later-and-it-s-still-an-amazing-game. It was also my personal experience of the game. But there is some disagreement; see Zack Waggoner's essay "Conf(us)(ess)ions of a Videogame Role-Player" in *Writing and the Digital Generation: Essays on New Media Rhetoric.*

[4] *Morrowind* can quite clearly be categorized as a "first person" game, in that the player controls a single character and views the world from that character's perspective; role-playing games in which a player controls a "party" might all be classified as "third person," though there are some distinctions that can be made. In *The Bard's Tale,* for example, the player creates and controls

a group of characters (and so it has a third-person feel), but the visual perspective is similar to what are considered "first person" games, with the player viewing the game world as though he were present in it; other "adventuring party" games like *Baldur's Gate* and *Ultima IV* begin with the player controlling a single character but gaining additional party members over the course of play; the perspective of those two games is not first person, but top-down/third person.

[5] *The Cambridge Dictionary of Philosophy, Second Edition,* ed. Robert Audi. Cambridge: Cambridge University Press, 1999, pg. 296.

[6] *Ibid,* pg. 297.

[7] Voegelin, *Israel and Revelation*, pp. 1-2:"The role of existence must be played in uncertainty of its meaning…Both the play and the role are unknown. But even worse, the actor does not know with certainty who he is himself."

[8] The adventuring party has largely been conjured up by the strength of Tolkien's storytelling in *The Fellowship of the Ring* – arguably the entire genre of fantasy role-playing games (and perhaps role playing games as a whole), from the paper and pencil *Dungeons and Dragons* to the computer driven *Morrowind*, owe their existence to Tolkien's imaginative vision. Undeniably the impetus to create (and play) such games in the genre's formative years owed a great deal to the desire to enter into Middle Earth in some way.

[9] A more recent classic of the genre, *Baldur's Gate*, effectively embellished the pattern by having the player roll up his own character and then join with other characters on his journey – they became part of the "party" without directly having been created by the player, and carried certain limitations to the player's ability to control them – the earlier *Ultima IV* used a similar scheme.

[10] In *Morrowind,* the moral dilemma element in character creation is optional, but anyone who played *Ultima IV* could hardly resist forming his character this way. Bethesda's *Fallout 3* features a similar character creation sequence as *Morrowind.*

[11] Thrasymachus argues alternately that justice is "the will of the stronger," and that injustice can be stronger and freer than justice, in Book I of *The Republic*, 338c and 334c; Glaucon carries on Thrasymachus' dispute by introducing the Ring of Gyges in Book II, which through its power to grant invisibility would allow a man to appear to be just while doing as he wills.

[12] One should note that after the completion of the narrative, *Morrowind* allows the player to keep playing, freed of any constraints to their actions that might have applied while they were attempting to finish the game.

[13] And how exceptional individuals are selected would itself present an existential dilemma.

[14] This might apply broadly to digital media as a whole. While many individuals seek to be outlandishly "authentic" with their online personas, putting their "best face" (or most extreme) on Facebook, one gets the sense that it is simply a "put on" – being authentic in the digital sense may allow people to remain anonymous in their material lives. In their dreams, all men are great – on Facebook, all people are "authentic." A shy, non-confrontational person might step into discussion rooms and hold forth mightily on all manner of topics. He may even begin to think that when he is doing so he is more his "authentic" self.

[15] For an example, see http://www.neoseeker.com/forums/5665/t504620-morrowinds-best-bases-houses/

[16] What is interesting about very early video games like Pac-Man, Asteroid, et al. is that there were theoretically infinite levels; one played until one lost. Early games like Pac-Man often had a "kill screen," when the game ended due to memory restrictions. It would be interesting to explore when and how game designers transitioned from this type of default "endgame" to game conclusions with victory screens or sequences (video games that were explicitly designed to come to a conclusion), but there is no time for it here.

[17] In this particular case, playing the game is a more rewarding experience than reading the

book. What's especially interesting about *Below the Root* is that the player's character never performs any actions very much out of scale with any non-player character; indeed the player's character can be quite weak in ability compared with other characters.

[18] There is no resurrection in *Morrowind* game play, so death signals the end of the story; this is perhaps the most obvious difference between the messianic theme of *Morrowind* and Christian messianism.

Making Gods:

The Nature and Media of Divinity in Apotheosis and Theosis

BY JOSHUA WISE

The practice of making men or women into gods is of an unknown antiquity. It may be that our oldest tales became legend and legend became myth, until the story of the tribal chieftain became the story of the sky god.[1] But if this is so, the time when it happened is hidden in the age of pre-written human experience. Perhaps echoes of it exist in the few tales we have of men and women who, having lived exceptional lives, ascend to sit in the seats of the gods after their deaths. Heracles and Dionysus, having been mortal men, are elevated to godhood in the classical Greek tradition.

But in recorded Western history we have striking records of mortals being declared gods in the early Roman empire.[2] The apotheosis of Julius Caesar, his adoptive son Octavian, known as Augustus, and his successors, are the classical examples of mortals being declared divine. The other glaring example, of course, is the Christian claim to the divinity of Jesus.

The world of *The Elder Scrolls* also contains those human beings who have become divine, most notably Talos, known as Tiber Septim, Dagoth Ur and the Tribunal, Vivec, Amalexia and Sotha Sil. But, as we

The practice of making men or women into gods is of an unknown antiquity. It may be that our oldest tales became legend and legend became myth, until the story of the tribal chieftain became the story of the sky god.[1] But if this is so, the time when it happened is hidden in the age of pre-written human experience. Perhaps echoes of it exist in the few tales we have of men and women who, having lived exceptional lives, ascend to sit in the seats of the gods after their deaths. Heracles and Dionysus, having been mortal men, are elevated to godhood in the classical Greek tradition.

But in recorded Western history we have striking records of mortals being declared gods in the early Roman empire.[2] The apotheosis of Julius Caesar, his adoptive son Octavian, known as Augustus, and his successors, are the classical examples of mortals being declared divine. The other glaring example, of course, is the Christian claim to the divinity of Jesus.

The world of *The Elder Scrolls* also contains those human beings who have become divine, most notably Talos, known as Tiber Septim, Dagoth Ur and the Tribunal, Vivec, Amalexia and Sotha Sil. But, as we will see, the process of apotheosis in the world that Bethesda has created, is significantly different than how apotheosis has been practiced in human history.

This article will consider what apotheosis means specifically in the Roman context, as well as what it means in the world of *The Elder Scrolls*. Specifically, the concept of divinity as well as the medium of divinization will be considered. Finally, a comparison of the concept of apotheosis with the Christian concept of Theosis will be explored in light of differing ideas of how divinity functions in the different models of Rome, *The Elder Scrolls* and Christianity.

Roman Apotheosis:
THE DIVINE POLITIC

Histories of Julius Caesar generally are not considered to be histories of a divine person in the modern world. Instead, despite the fact that the Roman Senate voted Caesar divine honors, declaring him to be among the immortal gods, we consider him a man like any other in the facts that he was born on a certain date, lived a certain amount of time and died. A linear accounting of Gaius Julius Caesar's life ends on the Ides of March. If it considers a human life to include its immediate aftermath, it may also include the eulogy of Mark Antony and the hunting down of the assassins. Perhaps it will mention that, upon the request of Octavian Caesar, the Roman Senate declared him divine, and may also affirm that at the games held in his honor a comet, believed to be the divine soul of Julius, appeared.

But that is all. Julius was dead, long live the Triumvers. After Actium, long live Augustus.

The tale ends because we do not generally affirm, that Julius truly became divine the day the Senate voted that he should be recognized as a god. In the end of Ovid's *Metamorphoses*, he declares that Julius is transformed into a star to sit among the divine ones. This is generally not considered a real event in the life of the man who was known for wearing his belt a little too loose for the stodgier older senators. A physical description of the man does not usually conclude with "and this is what Caesar looked like before he became a star."

The emphasis on this distinction here is made because it shows something of our modern conception of divinity. While much of modern western culture is somewhat skeptical about divinity, the idea that a man simply might become divine due to the statements of other men, is discounted as a rule. A group of people, regardless of who they are, saying, "this man is a god" carries very little weight to our modern minds.

However, it would be wrong to characterize the Roman understanding in this light. Modern people might look at the senators like they look at the British Parliament or the American Congress and see mortal men and women who can declare someone a god about as effectively as they can create a new color by voting on it. But the Romans did not see their senate merely as a group of men in a room, but as a expression of the very state in which they lived. And that state had a very complicated relationship with divinity.

The Roman understanding of his or her own city and how it related to the concept of divinity would be too much to go into here. Roma was, of course, a goddess; she was under the protection of the gods and, by the power of the gods, the people were who they were. Each crossroads was haunted by gods and every household populated by them. The city itself was founded by Romulus who himself was deified into the god Quirinus.[3]

Little to nothing was done without seeking the portents from the gods, either actively or passively. There were auspicious and inauspicious days to do most things. The whole world of the Romans was permeated by the gods. So when the Roman Senate voted divinity to Julius, it was understood as a mortal affirmation of a divine reality.[4]

If we skip down a generation to the Emperor Augustus, we find that his apotheosis was understood to be fitting due to the portents reported before and after his death. Famously, lightning struck one of his statues and melted the "C" from his name, leaving the word "Aesar." "C" in the Latin world meant 100, and Aesar in Etruscan meant "god." Augustus reportedly died one hundred days later.[5] Further, Tiberius, Augustus' successor, argued for his divinization in his Eulogy for his own adoptive father.

The reasons for these divinizations may appear to be to recognize the great works that a person accomplished in their lives. But even in the days of Augustus, this was seen to be false. In Ovid's *Metamorphoses*, the reason given for Julius' elevation to godhood is for Augustus to have a divine ancestor and predecessor. The divinity of Julius is in the service of the reign of Augustus. We can then see the same principle at work in Tiberius' request that Augustus should be divinized. Validation by a god for one's rule can be a very handy thing to have in the political realm.

Divinity for the Romans functioned in numerous capacities, but in the sphere of apotheosis, it seems to have functioned significantly as a means to a political end. As a correlate to its political end, we observe that it has a political origin. Divinity is conferred, in these cases, by the official apparatus of the state, the Roman Senate, and often arises from the acclamation of the state proper, the voice of the people.[6] The divinity of these figures then is tied to the state as an entity and subject to its whims and fluctuations. Should the state declare that such concepts of divinity were no longer recognized, then the status of the divine persons changes. Julius is no longer god, only a famous warrior and statesman.

MODELS OF DIVINITY

In the world of *The Elder Scrolls*, something quite different seems to be taking place with the five figures who are divinized. These fall into two general categories that will be considered separately. The first category, which contains the Tribunal of Morrowind and Dagoth Ur, involves the temporary participation in divine attributes by mortal beings. The second, which primarily focuses on Talos, or Tiber Septim, appears to involve the actual transformation of a mortal into the divine state. Each of these will be considered in turn, but first we must understand what is meant by divinity in the world of *The Elder Scrolls*.

The Ancient World

The concept of deity is a complicated one for any short study to tackle. The general descriptions of immortality, omniscience and omnipotence are not universally attested in pagan concepts of divinity. To be divine in the ancient world was perhaps to be able to contend with powers that existed above the immediate human sphere of influence. The sky god could wrangle thunder, the sea god the waves. Men and women, subject to these powers, saw that those who could control or contend with them were divine. Thus we find that Thor and Zeus both rule those powers that terrify humanity with the roar of thunder and the flashing bolt. Manawydan and Poseidon rule the waves to which the ships of sailors are subject. And for some, like the Greeks, even death itself is mastered by those who walk the Olympian slopes. But this was not so for all. Notably, the Norse and Egyptians had gods who died.

Divinity then seems to be, at least for mythopoeic cultures, that state of being in which one is master of the powers that master humanity. However, when the philosophers of Greece began to ask about divinity itself, new conclusions began to be drawn. The divine was not merely master of the sphere of humanity, but so far above it as to be outside of it. The Stoic god is beyond the being of the universe. Aristotle's god is one who, by being perfect, moves the universe in its desire to emulate the perfection. The Neo-Platonic One emanates the nous and the psyche in which time and space subsists.

In all of these systems, however, the concept of divinity is still tied to the world. The divine one is linked by a series of emanations or by a common mutual context (being itself) that allows the cosmos to perceive the divine in some way. A philosophically predicated divinity might be other, but it is not wholly other. Perhaps the god no longer has arms, legs and a beard, and his abode is not on a mountain, but it is still contextually linked to our world. Lightning may not flash because the irresistible hand of Zeus has hurled it, but the god is still, in some way, master, even if now a vastly disinterested master.

The Christian Distinction

The Christian distinction[7] was predicated on the affirmation of the man Jesus of Nazareth as God. The firm distinction between the Creator who made the world from nothing and needed nothing, and the creation which was wholly dependent on the Creator, allowed for the Creator to remain God and also become a human. Only one who was fully outside of the system, not one of the things in the universe, could become a human being and yet remain exactly the same.[8] Only by being wholly outside of creation could the second person of the Trinity remain wholly God and take on humanity. Something inside of order would need to either change its nature or simply appear to be human.

Divinity then, in the Christian context, became a state of being in which all finite predicates were insufficient. This was not simply because the idea of God and divinity got bigger. Instead, it could be said that it became truly "other." To be divine was now to be outside of the system for which we have words. The infinite God proposed by Gregory of Nyssa, and the God who is beyond being, spoke of by Pseudo-Dionysius the Areopagite, was not able to be measured by space because space was made by this God. God could be said "not to exist" because divinity made everything by which we define the word "existence." God is source of being, and therefore beyond it.[9]

Even today, the conflict in understanding the Christian idea of divinity lies in the meeting place between the old pagan concept of the divine being who rules over the powers that rule humanity and the newer idea of the One who stands outside of the created order and may access and adjust it at will.

Divinity in The Elder Scrolls

The myths of the world in *The Elder Scrolls* speak of the Serpent God Anu and his brother Padomay, who exist in relationship with each other. The first seems to represent order, and the second chaos. Where they interact and overlap, the created realms exist. From their interaction, the gods come forth, the Original Spirits. The two primordial powers bring forth the realm of Mundus and includes the world in which *The Elder Scrolls* games exist, Nirn, as well as Oblivion, and other realms.

The gods arise from the interaction of these basic realities, though no explanation is given as to how these two basic entities exist in relation to each other. In this way, the myth of *The Elder Scrolls* is very much like basic pagan mythologies that begin with the Sky, or Ginnungagap. There is already a stage set, already relationship without context or explanation.

The Aedra and Daedra arise from the conflict and are divine in the world of *The Elder Scrolls*. One of the gods comes forth and, with him, time exists. Others come forth from the interaction of the two basic powers, and are convinced by one of the gods, Lorkhan, to create Nirn. The legends of *The Elder Scrolls* games paint this creation in two different lights. The first is that of the "Mer," the elven races of the world and the second, of Humans. The first view is that Lorkhan tricked the other original spirits to create Mundus. And, in doing so, they lost much of their original power and divinity. The Original Spirits became the Aedra and Daedra, lesser beings than they once were. The Mer, who see themselves as descended from the Aedra, blame Lorkhan for their mortality. Humans, on the other hand, do not see themselves as descended from the gods and view their existence as owed entirely to the creation of Nirn by Lorkhan.

In either view, Lorkhan died in the process of creating Nirn. He gave his life so that the world might be created and by his sacrifice really became the one god to die truly.[10]

The whole mythical structure of *The Elder Scrolls* has an affinity to the structures generally called Gnostic belief systems. There is a primordial whole, or couple, that then begets beings of lesser divinity, until eventually the world is made through an act of desire or ignorance. Human spirits are trapped in their fleshly prisons and desire to arise to the spirit realm from whence they came.

But what is not clear is how the concept of divinity is really defined. We observe that it functions in degrees and that the Aedra and Daedra, while still mighty gods, are no longer as mighty as they once were. Through extraordinary circumstances, gods may actually die. The gods themselves arise from the two primordial powers, ostensibly deriving their divinity from these conflicting sources.

We are left with the impression that divinity in *The Elder Scrolls* functions as a basic framework for mythological power. General categories of function, such as control of the world's elements, responsibility for creation and explanation of identity, are all identifiable. The gods are responsible for the world as it is and give mortal beings a framework in which to understand their own identity.

The appropriation, then, of divinity in the world of *The Elder Scrolls* is of this framework. Whereas in the Roman system the process of apotheosis was a political one, the apotheosis of figures in the *The Elder Scrolls* is an entry into a life of power and unending life. However, the question remains open in any particular instance, whether this is simply a partaking in an external framework which conveys the attributes of divinity, or an actual change in nature. We will consider here the examples of the Tribunal and Tiber Septim.

The Tribunal and Dagoth Ur–Participation in Divinity

The three figures of the Tribunal, Vivec, Sotha Sil and Amalexia, are divine beings who rule over the land of Morrowind in the third major game of *The Elder Scrolls* series.[11] Their divinity is not by nature, however. Instead, by means more complicated than we will enter into in this essay, they received divinity by drawing it from an object called The Heart of Lorkhan. The Heart, which allegedly is the last remaining element of the god that created the world, was accessed through magical means to share its divinity with those who wielded certain artifacts. While the means of the transfer are especially characteristic of a fantasy world, the underlying concepts are particularly interesting to us here.

Divinity, as we have surmised, is a general framework which conveys or suggests certain attributes. The loss of these attributes is indicative of a lesser participation in the framework. Conversely, participation in the framework conveys these attributes to the level at which the person participates.[12]

As we have seen, participation in the framework of divinity is not a guarantee of continued participation. The Aedra lose some of their divinity through the creation of the world. The Tribunal, having acquired for themselves divinity through media which transfer divine attributes to them (the artifacts), also lose these attributes when the media are destroyed. The removal of the conduits of their power and immortality results in the removal of the results of that immortality.

Thus, the Tribunal participate in the divine framework by means of an external process that does not change their natures. They remain naturally mortal, returning to this state when the external power is withdrawn from them.

Tiber Septim

The apotheosis of Tiber Septim in *The Elder Scrolls* is far less transparent than that of the Tribunal. In the fiction of the game, there is some debate as to whether or not Tiber Septim, in fact, became the god Talos; we will, for the purposes of this essay, assume that the official account is accurate. At the end of a life of war, power, and rule, the man Tiber Septim who founded a line of Emperors, became revered as a god. His divine status appears to be more than simple affirmation since he appears in *Morrowind* as an aid to the player at an important moment.

However, with the dearth of information regarding the process of his divinization, we can say little about it except to assume that what we have concluded from other elements of the mythology of the world is also applicable to him. If Tiber Septim became the god Talos, then it follows that he began to participate in the divine framework in which all of the gods do. As he is worshipped among the other eight divines, we might guess that he, at least in some way, participates in divinity in the way that the others do.

When the Tribunal took divinity to itself, the Daedra Azura cursed them. However, there is no record of any rejection of Talos by the other nine. The rejection instead comes from the Aldmeri Dominion who reject the idea that a mortal could become a god. Thus, in *Skyrim*, the worship of Talos is outlawed by the White-Gold Concordat, a treaty between the Aldmeri Dominion and the Empire.

The rejection of Talos' deity is a political one, but therefore functions on a different level than that on which it was originally conveyed. The affirmation of deity by the Roman Empire is undone by the change in the political landscape. Even if we consider the attestation that the popular opinion was that Caesar was divine before his death, that view changed over time. Thus, the very entities which affirmed Caesar's deity also later denied that deity. Yet, with Talos, it seems that in some way he really assumed the deity shared with the other eight divines. No merely political power could then revoke that deity. It seems that only other acts or decrees of the divine in the world of *The Elder Scrolls* could, in fact, remove his apotheosis. This holds true when we consider how the Tribunal loses its deity, as it was conferred by the artifacts of Lorkhan, and revoked when they no longer conveyed it.

THEOSIS

In light of all of this, it is interesting to consider the Christian teaching of Theosis popular among the Eastern traditions of the Church. The teaching of Theosis, or deification, is the teaching that God somehow shares God's own self with humanity through the Incarnation of Jesus so completely that humanity itself becomes divine. The often repeated classical texts come from Irenaeus of Lyons and St. Athanasius of Alexandria, though we might also easily add texts from Gregory of Nyssa and Cyril of Alexandria and St. Augustine. "God became Human so that Humans might become God."

There are, of course, caveats to this happy trade. The traditional formulation of this teaching staunchly maintains that human nature remains human nature and that it becomes divine by partaking in the divine nature.[13] As partakers of the divine nature, the human being takes on the attributes of the divine, immortality, wisdom, power, love, goodness and more.[14] The transformation is one of attributes that align with God's attributes displayed in God's actions in the created world. However, there is not a participation in God's actual being or substance. To have God's substance would be to be God and while the Fathers speak in a way that alludes to this, it is only by an understanding of the term ,"God," with relation to creation that we are able to fully and firmly grasp what is meant.

For much of the Eastern Tradition that follows the writings and teachings of Gregory Palamas, the concept of the Divine Energies is central to understanding what Theosis means. The Divine Energies are God's actions in the universe which, while consistent with God's hidden nature, are expressed in limited and therefore in ways that are able to be categorized . Thus we see God's goodness in God's actions, but Goodness itself is a limited category which does not fully encompass God's own being which is far beyond our concept of Goodness.[15] By becoming aligned with and participating in these energies, the divine attributes of God's life are also communicated to us.

The principle of divinity then is not inherent to the human being in Theosis; it remains the three-person God who shares immortal life with those who will also share in humility, peace, forgiveness and ultimately death with Christ. We might say that life remains technically external to the human being, derived from another in a way similar to the divinity of the Tribunal in Morrowind. In fact, the similarity is somewhat striking as well, since both the Tribunal and Christianity rely on a god who has died. However, the distinction between Christian Theosis and the divinity of the Tribunal and Dagoth Ur is at least threefold.

First, the divinity of the Tribunal/Dagoth Ur is a stolen divinity. Lorkhan is not intentionally sharing his divine life with these four persons in order to share his identity to them. This is quite the opposite in Christianity, for Christ and the Spirit share the divinity of God with humanity in a way that identifies God with humanity.[16] There is a relationship between persons, not simply between natures. The debate concerning the nature/person in God within Christianity notwithstanding, we may safely say that God has a personal relationship with humanity predicated on God's free will. Lorkhan has no free will in having his divinity used by both Vivec and Dagoth Ur.

Second, the media of the communication of divinity are, in Morrowind, artifacts designed to harness the power as an object. Christianity, on the other hand, maintains that the media of communication for our divinity, the Sacraments, are not able to be manipulated like tools. There is not room here to go into a full theology of sacraments; however, we may say a few brief things. Sacraments are co-workings of God and humanity, but humanity may not simply command them to happen. The baptism of a person and the feeding of the congregation with the body and blood of Christ are works that we do in obedience to Christ, not merely of our own volition. These sacraments, done by both God and the Church, communicate the divinity of God to us, not by water and bread, but by God's own self communicated through the elements. The universally Catholic, Orthodox and Lutheran views[17] that the bread is flesh and the wine is blood are testimonies to the fact that the real medium of God's divinity is God. No other may give us the life of God but the Divine Three, the Divine One. There is no "hocus pocus" allowed.[18] The artifacts which transmit the divinity of Lorkhan to the Tribunal tap into the divinity of the god as an object accessible to them. This is due to the fact that, as we have observed, divinity is something which is not natural to the gods. Divinity is imparted to them and can be taken from them. The Christian God is not imbued with divinity, nor is divinity an aspect of the Christian God. Instead, the nature of God is not really distinguishable from the persons of God.[19]

Thirdly, the divinity shared with the Tribunal is lost. Because the media of communication are both external to the recipients and to the source of the divinity, the tools themselves may be destroyed or simply cease to work. This is exactly what happens in *Morrowind*. The gods become mortal again. But in Christian theology, the medium of divinity is the Divine. The sharing of the divine life with mortals is an irrevocable act by God. If one rises into eternal life, there is no question of falling away again.[20] The life that is given to humanity by God is truly its own because it is truly and wholly given. There is no power that can come between the life given and the one who receives the life. So closely are they identified that each and every person in it may say, "This life is mine because it is given to me." Yet the fact that this life is given is never lost sight of. In fact, the acknowledgement of the gift is one of the sine qua non of the receiving and possessing of the gift.[21]

CONCLUSIONS

When we consider the concept of divinization in these three contexts, that of the Roman, of the world of *The Elder Scrolls*, and of the Christian, we find that it is integral to our understanding to see clearly what the medium of divinization is. For the Roman state, it was the state itself. Its means were political as well as its ends. In Morrowind, the means of divinization are magical and, ultimately, instrumental. The end is also instrumental. The Tribunal rules in order to effect change in the relationship between the divine and the mortal.[22] In Christianity, the means and the end are personal. It is the divine relation of love that is shared with humanity and is played out in the kingdom preached by Christ. Love as Father, Son and Holy Spirit is shared with human persons to the end that they might live in the kind of love that God is. The life of God which makes men and women gods is eternal and thus is unassailable, which neither the state, nor the artifacts in *The Elder Scrolls*, can claim.

WORKS CITED

Chalupa, Ales. "How did Roman Emperors Become Gods? Various Concepts of Imperial Apotheosis". *Studies of the Ancient World.* 6-7/2006-2007, 201-207.

Dio Cassius. *Roman History.*

St. Irenaeus. *Adversus Haereses.*

Ovid, *Metamorphoses.*

Sokolowski, Fr. Robert. *God of Faith and Reason: Foundations of Christian Theology.* Washington D.C.: Catholic University of America Press, 1995.

Sturluson, Snorri. *The Prose Edda.*

Endnotes

[1] The reverse process may be seen in the introduction to the *Snorra Edda* in which the Norse gods are declared to be men from the ancient world whose fame had won them worship in the northern lands. This was done by the author ostensibly to show that the work he was undertaking to write was in no way an offense to the living God.

[2] The Egyptian, Ancient Near Eastern, and Asian practices of declaring rulers divine will here be bracketed both for space as well as relevance. The influence of the Roman Empire is obvious in several aspects of *The Elder Scrolls* games, and especially with regard to the topic at hand.

[3] Ovid, *Metamorphoses*, Book 14, 812-828.

[4] The people themselves are reported to have worshipped Julius as a god even before his death and apotheosis, and the titles given to Julius before his death essentially amounted to a divine status as well, Ales Chalupa, "How did Roman Emperors Become Gods? Various Concepts of Imperial Apotheosis", Studies of the Ancient World 6-7/2006-2007, 201-207.

[5] Dio Cassius, 56.29.

[6] Chalupa, "Imperial Apotheosis", 202.

[7] Expressed well by Fr. Robert Sokolowski, *God of Faith and Reason: Foundations of Christian Theology*, (Washington D.C.: Catholic University of America Press, 1995).

[8] A very small hint of this principle can be found in the lived experience of we who play video games taking control of a game character and yet remaining what we are. This analogy must not be followed too far, however, without considerable philosophical work. See, as an introduction to this idea, my other essay in this book.

[9] Thus we have the theological concept of the analogy of being.

[10] Unless of course the god Shor who rules over Sovngarde (see Jacob Torbeck's essay in this collection). At this point, as at many points, the data is conflicting in the in-world explanations of *The Elder Scrolls* series.

[11] Their enemy, Dagoth Ur, has the same relationship to divinity that the members of the Tribunal do, for all practical purposes. Thus he may be read into the same framework.

[12] It may not be appropriate to say, however, that an increase in the attributes themselves indicates a participation in the framework. An increase of power, for example, does not seem to automatically convey some divinity to the person.

[13] The reference to 2 Peter 1:4, however, only became often used in the discussion of Theosis with Cyril of Alexandria.

[14] Irenaeus Adv. Her. 3.20.

[15] This should not be confused with an idea that God is "beyond good and evil" in a sense of being "above" the ideas of Goodness and Evil and somehow either encompassing or rejecting both. Our very best ideas of goodness are absolutely more representative of God than our ideas of Evil, but gloriously, not exhaustive of God's actual goodness, and thus our term "goodness" is insufficient.

[16] The God who refers to Himself as "the God of Abraham, Isaac, and Jacob" and "The God of Israel" ties His identity to history and to people. This is either done in a "real" or a "rational" way. If "real" then the identity of God is really tied to humanity such that to know God at all is to know the God of Abraham. If "rational" then it is possible to know God and not necessarily know Him as the God of Abraham. For humans this is merely theoretical as in human history, God has come as the God of Abraham. But for other beings, angels, aliens, sentient beings of other realities, the identify of God as the God of Abraham may be a real question. Must we know the history of the human race to fully know God? This extends into eschatological and ontological questions, some of which are addressed briefly in my other essay here.

[17] These three traditions holding universally to this view. Other traditions, like my own, may or may not hold to this view.

[18] Whether or not the term "Hocus Pocus" really derives from the term "Hoc est corpus" is debated. However, the erroneous idea that we may simply, by saying some words and doing some actions, command God to be present, is tidily summed up by this phrase.

[19] Thus we reject what we understand to be the Thomistic view that the divine nature gives rise to three persons. Instead, we maintain a view more in line with the East, which sees the Godhead as resident in the Father that is perfectly shared with the Son and Spirit.

[20] This is not, as one might think, because the human will is then "fixed" and no longer free. Instead, the Christian understanding has often been that the eternal life frees the will to fix itself on the most desirable and wonderful object it can, God. No longer bound by a darkened understanding, or the desire for lesser goods, the human will is free from its slavery to false desires. One might compare this with an addict being freed from the love of heroine to instead love what is truly good in life. Someone freed from the addiction, so that they never will feel the desire, in fact are so cured that they could no longer feel the desire for the drug, would never speak of their will being no longer free, but wholly free from the slavery of addiction. This is a glimpse as what Christianity means at the freedom of the will in eternal life.

[21] Irenaeus, Contra Her., 3.20.

[22] For more on this, see Joshua Gonnerman's essay in this volume.

DEATH AND THE LIFE AFTER:

Eschatology in *The Elder Scrolls V: Skyrim*

BY JACOB W. TORBECK

Mythopoeia have always been a way in which cultures have mixed entertainment with philosophy and theology. By couching real questions inside of fictional mythologies, the authors of such works inoculate those who engage them against the more dangerous or unappealing aspects of such problems so that they may be worked out surreptitiously in the minds of the audience members. For example,

"In Homer's human, all too human, depiction of the gods there is a touch of irony, and a suggestion of rebellion against the peevish caprices of the higher powers. In Greek tragedy this incipient revolt is actually declared. The tragedians' *deus ex machina* gives dramatic form to a contestation or denial of the actual world and its gods. Were they truly divine, they would intervene as saviors and establish justice in the city... Those attitudes also generated a program for human emancipation from the traditional powers that be."[1]

The Elder Scrolls series stands in this artistic tradition of mythopoeia; indeed, the fantasy role-playing game genre is mythopoeic by convention

-- heroes must become such against the backdrop of cosmic drama and epic struggle against forces of oppression, destruction and death, in many cases using these same anti-heroic forces to thwart the antagonist and win the day, for whatever purpose. While other essays in this volume focus on the process of becoming a hero or creation myths, and so on, this examination focuses on the ultimate force and means of achieving many video game goals: death. The problem of death occupies a central place in the psyche of conscious mortal beings. In the real world, ideas about and theologies of death are as diverse and varied as the cultures who create them. In life, we understand death primarily by means of how it claims others and, in a manner, removes them from the world, and also by grappling with the immense uncertainty of what might happen to us when our body ceases to live. Death has been seen as the end of consciousness, the end of one incarnation among many (in preparation for the next) and the beginning of an eternal afterlife, with a plethora of values and hermeneutics to make sense of each conceptualization.

The Elder Scrolls presents a world rich with fictional people and their motivations, fears and values and a mythology that almost regularly breaks into the "real lives" of the fictional populace of Nirn, the world of mortals. Included in this world are competing pantheons of powerful gods and demi-gods, working -- whether overtly or in the shadows -- to maximize their power and influence and inviting mortals to choose sides by committing to an ultimate destiny, an eternal afterlife in one of the many planes of existence beyond the Mundus, the mortal plane. These destinies vary according to the culture and values of the people who are to look forward to them with eschatological hope, sometimes diverging widely from real known religions, despite drawing inspiration from our world's millennia of recorded myths and faith traditions.

In the similarities, as well as the differences, *The Elder Scrolls* presents not merely one, but many detailed eschatological mythoi within its greater mythopoeia. For the scholar of myth, religion, the human sciences at large, or even just an introspective gamer, the game series provides an interesting opportunity to reflect on those "last things" that have always mystified humans and fascinated the imagination, death, heaven, and hell. While it could be argued that both *Oblivion* and *Skyrim* are, in their main storyline, primarily concerned with the end of the world, for the sake of this essay, our examination will focus on eschatology in *Skyrim*, especially that eschatology which is explicitly the source of the game's plot: the conflict with Alduin, the World-Eater.

Basic Cosmological Structure in View of Death and Eternal Life

Engaging the last things is never easy. Indeed, on the subject of eschatology, it has been said when we consider what we think we know, we are often reduced to silence. Even in *Skyrim*, in which the Dragonborn is privileged to travel between planes of existence and witness the existence of souls in the afterlife, the common person engages such questions in much the same way that you and I would: with a blend of traditions, rituals, anxieties and hopes bound together in some degree of cohesion by religious belief and practice that only sometimes is the center or focus of their daily life. Outside the fourth wall, on this side of reality, a simple playthrough of *Skyrim* only reveals limited information. Much like religious or philosophical knowledge outside of video games, in *Skyrim*, such knowledge is gained through conversations with people you encounter as well as the study of the many texts on the matter scattered throughout the game. Because such knowledge is not always discovered, even in a thorough playthrough, before we begin a more intense dialogue about the eschatological themes engaged in the game world, it is useful to first sketch the cosmological landscape in which *Skyrim* takes place.

Aetherius as Heaven

Perhaps in the minds of most races of Nirn is the hope or expectation that when they die, their soul will be separated from their body and soar by unknown channels to Aetherius, the realm of pure magicka. Aetherius is the continual source of creation, whence the Aedra came, whence order comes to the universe by means of physical laws and whence the life-sustaining forces of the world and even the sun flow.

As *Skyrim* opens, the priestess at Helgen commends the souls of those to be executed to Aetherius in the name of the eight divines, those called upon previously by Lokir to save them.[2] This is true regardless of the race of the Dragonborn, leading us to believe perhaps that all peoples of Skyrim see Aetherius as a favorable destination, that the priestess believes all peoples see Aetherius as a favorable destination, or that the priestess only knows of one place to which to commend souls.

The very notion of "the heavens" as paradisiacal is linked to the symbolic force of that which is "above" or "higher" to express completion of existence.[3] In *The Elder Scrolls*, other planes of existence are *actually* perceived in the sky. Aetherius is visible through Oblivion, which is the dark void surrounding Nirn, in a way analogous to outer space. The stars, including the sun, called "Magnus," are actually the realm of Aetherius shining through points where, during the creation of the Mundus, the Aedra, Magnus and his Aedric followers, the Magna Ge, punctured the border between Aetherius and Oblivion, signifying powerful bridges between the heavens and Nirn. The world of Skyrim, however, is not a world where such realms cannot be reached. Indeed, while an almost impossibly difficult feat, exceptional travelers have visited the realms beyond Nirn, the plane of mortals. In the real world, travels to realms beyond physical existence, if they exist,[4] are beyond the capacity of science to achieve.[5] It is perhaps by revelations from those who have traveled the planes, or maybe because of superstitions grown up within cultures, that Aetherius is thought to have various subplanes within it -- Sovngarde being the chief example given to us in *Skyrim*.

Sovngarde and Feast as Aetherial Eucharistic Eschaton

Sovngarde, which in Scandinavian languages translates roughly to a "resting place,"[6] is the afterlife for valiant Nords, in some ways analogous to Asgard in the *Eddur* and sagas of Old Norse mythology. Central to the landscape of Sovngarde is the Hall of Valor, the eternal mead hall, reminiscent of Valhalla where, in Norse mythology, Odin takes the fallen from the battlefield to enjoy eternal revelry in the form of drinking, singing and brawling while they await the final battle, Ragnarök, at the end of time. Though this aspect of *Skyrim's* cosmology is evocative of Norse mythology, it differs in important ways that will be elucidated as this investigation continues.

Sovngarde is presented as the house of eternal revelry in the afterlife for all valiant Nords, as stated in the in-game book, *Sovngarde, A Re-examination,*

"It is time for Nords to learn the truth. Eternal life can be theirs, without the need to spend an entire mortal life in vain pursuit of something completely unattainable. In the end, all valiant Nords can enter Sovngarde. Dismemberment, decapitation or evisceration seems a small price to pay for the chance to spend an eternity in Shor's wondrous hall."[7]

For the Nord, it matters not so much the manner of one's living, but the manner of one's dying. A valiant death in battle grants the Nordic warrior the possibility of entering Shor's hall, so long as they can prove their worthiness to his shield-brother, the god Tsun, who stands guard at the whale-bone bridge to the Hall of Valor.

Much like in the Christian tradition and others, those who pass Tsun and enter are given open society and communion: an eternal feast and revelry. Joseph Ratzinger contends that the fundamental act of paradise is seen best in view of one's anthropological starting point.[8] Nordic heaven, then, might be better understood if we ask, "What is it to be a Nord?" We may also glean insight from the obvious parallel to the "source and summit" of the Catholic faith, the Eucharist, which draws upon the memory of the Jewish Passover and looks forward to an eternal banquet in the heavenly kingdom.

The question, "What is it to be a Nord?" is likely as complex as a more common question, "What does it mean to be human?" Certainly, not all Nords are warriors, but the warrior tradition runs deep in the blood of Nords and warriors are among the most honored people in Skyrim. The Companions, Skyrim's local adventurers' guild, celebrate this by engaging in travels and adventures that inspire skalds to sing of their deeds and celebrate together in their hall by feasting and brawling, almost sacramental precursors to the paradise that would await them, should they die in battle.[9] Values are almost too apparent when interacting with the Companions and even some other Nords: honor, courage, strength, loyalty and fraternity are all celebrated in Nordic tradition and the eternal celebration in Sovngarde seems not only for the pleasure of the feast for its own sake, but to eternally commemorate these virtues in the company of heroes whose values align -- in the Hall of Valor, even old enemies come together to toast at the long table.

The tradition of table-fellowship and the honor of being among such great heroes of Nordic culture makes Sovngarde a desirable afterlife for many. Created by Shor as a place where their cultural values could be celebrated, it also came to be the source of those values through the tales of warriors going to afterlife in its hallowed hall. Irenaeus of

Lyons elucidates this point when speaking of the Eucharist: "Our way of thinking is attuned to the eucharist; and the eucharist in turn confirms our way of thinking."[10] Shor's creation of Sovngarde to honor warriors past, present and future could be characterized in some ways as similar to the creative imagination of Jesus, who established the sacrament by drawing the memorial of the Old Testament priest Melchizedek, the feast of Passover and the manna in the desert into a new covenantal meal, filling it with new meaning by his passion and sacrificial death and inviting those who would take up the cup with him to be imbued not only with hope of things to come, but with his imagination as well.[11]

The Christian Eucharistic feast was named by Vatican II "the source and summit of the life of the Church."[12] As the source, hope for the feast in heaven is renewed as the church regularly proclaims the death of the Lord until his second coming, and re-presents the sacrificial love of Christ to God and the believers as food and drink for the journey are made a sign or sacrament of the broken body and blood of the suffering savior.[13] As summit, it provides a height toward which the church looks into the future, anticipating what is to come in its fullest realization: It is promised in the book of Revelation that Christ awaits the faithful in a heavenly feast, and the old order of adversity, sin and death is overthrown.

The metaphor of feasting for being in God's presence is singled out for its particular appropriateness in the work of Thomas Aquinas, who says that "taste attains what is present in an interior way. Now God is neither distant from us nor outside us... and so the experience of the divine goodness is called tasting."[14] This has been developed further by John Paul II, in that "the Eucharist is a straining towards the goal, a foretaste of the fullness of joy promised in Christ..." that for the believer grants a participation here and now in the heavenly feast, wherein the "'secret' of the resurrection'" is *digested*.[15] Not only are the faithful attuned to and confirmed by their Eucharistic transformation, they are enlightened and transformed by it.

What happens after the end of time is a matter of speculation for both the Nordic heroes and the Christian. Christians are promised a bodily resurrection and a new world of harmony to live in forever; the altar-table of the Eucharist represents not only the sacrifice of Christ, but also an invitation to eternal communion. In that vein, Nords in Sovngarde may never cease feasting, brawling and singing, although three ancient heroes are allowed to break from the revelry to assist the Dragonborn against Alduin. In the ingame book, *The Doors of Oblivion*, the planar traveler Morian Zenas seems to the author to fade into bliss when he discovers his paradise in the Daedric plane of Apocrypha. Perhaps after all things, the revelry of the Hall of Valor will fade back into Aetherius and all will return to the pure magickal creative source of life... for the fictional populace of *The Elder Scrolls* universe, it is unknown. However, as alluded to above, not all Nords are aware that a courageous death can earn them passage to an eternity full of mirth and free from boredom. The cosmos of *Skyrim* has myriad alternate planes of existence for those whose fortune or lack thereof takes them down other paths.

The Void and Oblivion as Hell

If Aetherius and its sub-regions, such as Sovngarde, are heavens, does that make the Void, the vast darkness which surrounds Nirn, *The Elder Scrolls'* version of hell? Or would that designation be more properly reserved for the planes of Oblivion? A direct parallel with world religions is not possible, but certain themes appear that color our reading of the Void and its extension, Oblivion, as hellish domains.

The Void is ruled over by the primordial god Sithis (also called Padomay), who instigated with Anu the conflict that led to the creation of the Aedra and whose blood solely gave life to the Daedra, who represents utter nothingness, and is appeased by death and suffering.[16] Worshipers of Sithis believe that the souls of those they kill go to the Void and what this might mean to that soul is a matter of grim speculation. Does being consigned to drift in nothingness result in annihilation? Perhaps.

Then again, perhaps not. The planes of Oblivion are extensions of the Void, not merely surrounding the other planes like the Void does, but coterminous with the Mundus. This hybrid realm serves as home to the Daedra and each of the sixteen planes are ruled over by a Daedric prince, some of which seem taken straight from the images of Satan seen on medieval tapestries. Diverse in size and environment, each has the characteristics of its ruler.

The planes of Oblivion play an interesting role in the eschatological cosmology of *The Elder Scrolls*. Daedra worshippers, in their fidelity to the Daedric prince they serve, upon death can be taken to that prince's holdings in Oblivion, for better or worse. Lycanthropes, for example, are taken by Hircine to his Hunting Grounds to participate eternally in the great hunt, while devotees of Hermaeus Mora drift through the infinite library of Apocrypha seeking knowledge in death as they did in life. In some ways, these planes resemble Sovngarde, as the spirits of the departed are perpetually occupied in a manner like unto their nature. Indeed, in some ways, some Daedric planes sound more heavenly than Sovngarde -- Moonshadow, the home of Azura, is too beautiful to behold with mortal eyes. In the in-game tome, *The Doors of Oblivion*, planar traveler Morian Zenas relays that he went "half blind" when he visited the beautiful realm.

There is a much darker side to Oblivion, however, in realms that much more resemble the hellish landscapes we often imagine eternal damnation to look like. From his realm of Coldharbour, which resembles a post-apocalyptic Nirn, Molag Bal delights in the domination of the mortal races and, to that end seeks to claim souls, presumably to torture and degrade. The Daedric Prince of Coldharbour is not above using violent coercion to claim these souls, as in the case of a Boethian priest the Dragonborn is asked to find and later subdue in *Skyrim*. The priest is tortured until he renounces his allegiance to Boethiah and pledges his fealty to Molag Bal, so that Bal may claim his soul in Oblivion when it proceeds there after his imminent death. In this case, the priest's soul was consigned to Molag Bal as a result of the priest's own action. As Karl Rahner put it, death is "the fruit of a final, free, and absolute decision growing out of time itself,"[17] from which Anthony Kelly elaborates, "Hell is a theological symbol of the sinner's self-chosen ultimate fate."[18] Elsewhere in his works, Rahner states that "everyone must say to himself or herself: 'I can be lost only through my own freedom.'"[19] In *Skyrim*, however, this is not always so. A far more violent possibility exists in the world of *The Elder Scrolls*, which could potentially trump salvific acts of devotion, such as a Nord's valiant death or lifelong service to Arkay.

An afterlife in Aetherius or another plane can be denied extrinsically by the actions of others. Enchantment in *Skyrim* (and *Oblivion*) requires the harnessed power of a captured soul. Most enchanters harness the souls of non-sentient creatures, those outside of the designations of mer or man. Although it widely viewed as a crime, some enchanters and necromancers nevertheless use black soul gems to trap the souls of persons for their private use as a power source or currency, preventing the person's soul from going to its destined afterlife. Some creatures, such as dremora, also have the ability to trap souls. In either case, the trapped soul is doomed to spend eternity in the Soul Cairn, a plane of Oblivion, where they are subject to everlasting torment and it is speculated they are used for currency, food or perhaps both by the plane's rulers, the Ideal Masters.[20]

Alduin the World-Eater

It is against the background of competing, and sometimes threatening afterlives that we can begin to situate the story of *Skyrim*. As the story begins, the Dragonborn, not yet knowing of his identity as such, is condemned to death for crossing the border illegally. The priestess at Helgen, where the Dragonborn is to be executed, invokes the help of the divines in guiding the souls of the prisoners to a pleasant afterlife in Aetherius, in a manner familiar to many religious traditions.[21] Just before the axe would fall, however, a dragon, thought by all but a few to be mythic or extinct, incinerates the city, allowing the Dragonborn to escape in the chaos.

It is not long, however, before the Dragonborn learns of his (or her) identity and also that of the dragon, Alduin, called the "firstborn of Akatosh" and the "World-eater," the herald and instrument of the apocalypse. The presence of a dragon at the end of the world might immediately call to mind the Christian book of Revelation, wherein the dragon establishes a worldly empire and gives authority to beasts and demands worship.[22] The ingame tome *Varieties of Faith in the Empire,* however, alludes to Alduin as the harbinger of not only the world ending (in his flames), but a new world's beginning. This concept of cyclic eschatology is seen in the Norse *Eddur.* In the Poetic Edda, the dragon Niðhöggr, who is also mentioned previously as gnawing at the base of the world tree (representing forces of destruction), heralds Ragnarök, the battle at the end of the world which not only ends in the world's being consumed by fire, but also the birth of a new world with a new people.[23]

Alduin's status as "World Eater" would be terrifying enough to the people of Skyrim, but in addition, he has resurrected the dragons in what seems not to be a plan of total remaking, but subjugation and destruction. Alduin's initial banishment had come about because he forsook his divine role as the World-Eater and broke in upon time to claim Nirn for himself and his dragons over and against all other races, which he saw as inferior. During the time when dragons ruled Skyrim, a Nordic religion rose up around the worship of the Nords' dragon masters, complete with devoted dragon-priests and their cadre of loyal attendants who believed the messianic return of Alduin would herald their resurrection from the dead. In preparation for this "second coming," an idea very familiar to the Christian imagination, the dragon-priests buried themselves in tombs along with their attendants. They would rise from their slumber as the undead *draugr* to perform rituals that sustained the dragon-priest, who slumbered in a special hibernation-like state while they awaited Alduin's return. This sort of burial practice, where followers and attendants are interred with the privileged classes, can be found across cultures from ancient Egypt to China and beyond. The worldly hope that those who served in life will continue to accompany the deceased as servants in the beyond is a reality in the game, made real by magic.

Christian eschatology turns this sort of expectation on its head, promising that those who take it upon themselves to serve in life will be great in the coming kingdom, becuase "the first will be last." Alduin's messianic promise can be understood in this way as anti-Christic -- the logic of authority among dragons in *The Elder Scrolls* is that power is truth. The ability to assert truth, or dominance, is seen by dragons and those they follow as a natural sign of superiority in the natural and supernatural order. The old draconic dominance fell apart when Alduin's cruelty became enough to provoke rebellion. Historic themes repeat when the

Imperials, who revere Akatosh, the Dragon of Time, and have imposed the Imperial Cult as an official religion, revering Akatosh, who represents everlasting legitimacy, as chief of the eight divines. The Empire is viewed as crumbling by the Stormcloak rebellion, who rebel *in part* as a reaction against the ban on the worship of Talos, who represents the ascendant potential of the mortal being (as he is Tiber Septim ascended)[24] and because he is so revered, threatened to overshadow Akatosh, a symbol not only of enduring legitimacy, in general, but the Empire's legitimacy, in particular.

The messianism of Alduin offers a much more overtly violent eschatology, wherein the oppressed remain thus, and the powerful are rewarded with still more power.[25] The politics of eschatology are discussed by Joseph Ratzinger in his influential text *Eschatology: Death and Eternal Life,* as being intimately related to the felt link between death and justice in the *polis,* or community. The revolt and rise of a hero are explained by Ratzinger, who speaks of the critique of the powers that be:

"Were they truly divine, they would intervene as saviors and establish justice in the city. Such attitudes, thus anticipated in a mythopoeic worldview, took on the explicit expression of a rational critique in the work of the Sophists. Those attitudes also generated a program for human emancipation from the traditional powers that be. What took the place of the latter was natural law -- understood, however, simply as the right to self-assertion of the stronger party. This development was to some extent prefigured in the Homeric figure of Odysseus.

But when trust in being and community is undermined in this way, and the individual's own advantage becomes the only lodestar, the bonds of community cannot hold. The spiritual crisis of the fifth and sixth centuries before Christ was also the political crisis of ancient Hellas."[26]

Ratzinger is speaking of the Hellenistic move away from a culture of myth and, if we apply his text with a direct and literal hermeneutic, it makes no sense in Skyrim, where supernatural powers really do exist and interact with history. A more flexible link between politics and eschatology must be employed.

In Skyrim, what we see is a rejection of the god of destruction, Alduin, when his divine right to rule was challenged. Without his divine right, an appeal to natural law meant only that a stronger being could usurp him. Stronger beings emerged and, with the aid of an Elder Scroll, banished Alduin forward in time. Alduin's return from banishment fittingly ends when, according to prophecy, misrule spreads across the world and kings are cast from their thrones. The political crisis heralds a spiritual and, indeed, existential crisis for all those on Nirn and even those in Sovngarde.

Many (if not most) of the people in Skyrim often do not look to the after-life, but rather find security in the cycle of life and death, which Ratzinger calls "a contented this-worldliness, a desire for fulfillment in the richness of a long life and continued existence in one's children and their posterity."[27] Eternal bliss seems a distant reality and an uncertain one, as according to ingame manuscripts, relatively few Nords are aware of the promise of Sovngarde. It is in situations of danger and desperation, rather than the old myths of divine assistance come flooding back to the forefront of the mind and the gods are invoked and pleaded with, if not for a safe return to the comfort of *this* life, then an afterlife in Aetherius. Alduin's return threatens the existing world, but in addition the World-Eater has found something that had alluded Nordic adventurers for millennia: a portal to the Nordic afterlife of Sovngarde.

After the Dragonborn forces Alduin to flee for his life, he runs to Sovngarde to lick his wounds and regain his strength by feasting on souls travelling down the misty paths of the Nordic paradise toward the Hall of Valor. This presents an imminent existential threat to all Nords - should they oppose Alduin, not only will their death be assuredly swift, but the promise of an afterlife is a promise not of the heaven they would have merited in their valiant deaths, but of a second death to nothingness, their soul consumed and absorbed while an eternal paradise lies within view. In the terrifying wake of the World-Eater, security in the cycle of life is disrupted and resistance is rendered more threatening than cowed submission. Thus eschatological hope is radically threatened.

Alduin's ability to consume the souls of the valiant dead again is reminiscent of the dragon of Ragnarök, Níðhöggr, who feeds on the corpses of the slain and carries them over the battlefield in his jaws.[28] The Poetic Edda, however, promises new beginnings after Ragnarök; The dead-god Baldr is resurrected and an era of humanity begins anew from Lif and Lifthrasir (*Life* and *Desiring-Life*), thereby giving hope to the ancient Norse that even after a terrible "end," life continues. Indeed, this is not merely a comfort for the eschatological future, but it speaks to the tragedies that break into the everyday lives of human persons: there is hope in hardship, not all is lost, people carry on, even from the brink of utter ruin and annihilation. Alduin offers quite the opposite... rather than a new beginning, his unmaking serves his own purposes of re-establishing his own superiority on Nirn.

The Self and the Adversary in the Eschaton

Alduin's deviation from his prescribed divine role as the herald of the Eschaton caused his initial banishment forward in time. Anthony Kelly situates deviation from the cycle of death and life as an embrace of the illusory sense of life, pretending "to exist to the extent of my planning and control." His characterization becomes even more fitting as he elucidates that such a pretense "evokes a sense of the individual as an ego somehow circling the planet in some form of deathless incarnation in a self-expressive project... but any life project, constructed in this way, is vulnerable. The larger world constitutes a threat... the 'vital lie' of character formed through the fear of death begins to hear the voice of a vital truth."[29]

The World-Eater's character seems not to be formed by the fear of his own death, but rather by the fears of others. As a god-like being (or perhaps merely a created dragon gifted with an eternal task),[30] the "first born of Akatosh" thinks himself superior to the order of Nirn and the cosmological structure facilitated by the primordial deities and facilitated by the Aedra and the Daedra. He is, in a manner of speaking, the adversary. Not just the adversary in the sense of being the game world's antagonist, but his role in the story seems to draw heavily on the character of Satan from Christian myth and scripture. Alduin's seizure of his own destiny and subsequent assertion of his venerability and dominance as a superior being is attested to in the Ancient Nordic tombs and evokes in the Western mind the tale of Lucifer. The highest angel of the heavens, Lucifer, unsatisfied with his god-given task and status as highest among the messengers of God, departed from his ordained purpose as the bearer of divine light, overstepped his boundaries and, in doing so, was banished.[31] He and his angels set about subverting worship of the One God and, in the eschaton, are finally cast into the pit, after which there is a heavenly banquet.[32]

It does seem that Alduin succeeded in instituting himself as an aspect of Akatosh, at least in the tombs of the Dragon Priests, as the ancient imagery in which the gods are symbolized by animals has only one dragon god, the god of destruction and chief of the pantheon. He is also banished, though not by the Aedric pantheon, but by mortals, who with the help of an Elder Scroll, cast him into the Fourth Age to be slain by the last Dragonborn. After this entry into the heavenly feast in Sovngarde's Hall of Valor is possible again for valorous Nords slain in battle. The presence of such a narrative in *Skyrim* demonstrates the convenience and/or the effectiveness of (predominantly Norse and Christian, here) religious apocalypticism in dealing with questions of struggle and death. It also possibly confirms the truth of Jürgen Habermas's thesis that "For the normative self-understanding of modernity, Christianity has functioned as more than just a precursor or catalyst," it undergirds, constitutes and co-determines Western religious thought to the extent that its narratives infiltrate even modern mythopoeia that are designed rather to resemble pagan epics.[33]

Psychologically and philosophically speaking, Alduin's rebellion can be seen as an act of self-assertion against the limitless "Other," represented by the Aedra, the people of Nirn, and finally the Dragonborn. Self-yielding, however, is what enabled the Aedra to empower the world with their life-giving spirits. In regard to self-making as a destructive path, Kelly claims that "without this self- yielding... the only valid position is nihilism... Any intimation of the infinite, any responsibility to what is other and outside my autistic purpose and control, is illusory... [Soskice] wittily describes the intrinsic autism of the nihilistic position as, 'If I can't be God, I don't want to play.'"[34] Alduin does not have much choice in the matter; in his attempt to play the part of a god, he is "removed from the game," as it were, when the Dragonborn banishes him once and for all, consigning him, should he ever return, only to his task as the prophesied World-Eater that initiates Nirn's death and rebirth in fire. The Dragonborn's story is left open, however. Whether he will become self-yielding or self-asserting, and what kind of future and afterlife he chooses is an open question up to the player, as *Skyrim's* quest system and additional content provide the possibility for various kinds of experimentation in role-play.

Concluding Reflections

The experience of *Skyrim* as *mythopoeia* inoculates the player against the real-life implications of questions that, for many people, present themselves uncomfortably in times of tragedy or mere existential angst.[35] The experience of engaging the narrative is valuable in enabling us to think, even if at a shallow level, about the awkward facts of death, afterlife and concern for oneself and others beyond the bounds of death.

Nevertheless, certain major differences between world religions and *Skyrim*'s mythic eschatology prevail. In contemporary world religions, the idea of redemptive violence is generally decried except in the purely spiritual sense of love and life winning out over hate and death; while in *Skyrim*, violence is the chief means of fulfilling the requirements of the main quest and, in its mythopoeia, achieving entrance to the Nordic afterlife.[36] Not only this, but the Nordic heaven of Sovngarde, taken from its context, would constitute an idol for Jean-Luc Marion and William Desmond; "an idol is a human projection... designed to reflect back on us what we are."[37] In short, that's what Shor made Sovngarde to be -- Sovngarde is the eternal celebration of *Nordic* heroism, divorced from the suffering and boredom of mortal life. Anthony Kelly would hope that each person would look not to an idol, but an icon, backlit with a *divine* light emanating from the source and sustainer of being, that exists not merely to communally and eternally celebrate the values of a beloved people, but to transform them into perfect likenesses of that divine icon.[38] The difference is, of course, in where the source of values ultimately originates. Though the promise of eternal reward is for many a catalyst for valuing and living out particular concepts, in *Skyrim*, Shor honors values of his beloved Nords by creating an eternal mead hall for them. By contrast, the Christian must be conformed to the other-worldly values of the kingdom of God and the Buddhist must learn to free themselves from worldly attachments in order to enter Nirvana.

Finally, the overthrow of the adversary Alduin and the restoration of the Nordic afterlife leave the Dragonborn hero with an open world in which to act out (or not) the implications of whatever spiritual insights have been gleaned from an encounter with the World-Eater. Depending upon one's playstyle, any number of possible lives and afterlives are open to the Dragonborn,[39] and nearly any degree of heroism or villainy. Is the Dragonborn substantially changed? After coming face to face with the end of the world, will the savior of Skyrim realize that "the Voice should be used for the worship and glory of the gods, not for the glory of man," or use it in some ways to exert his own ego, echoing the power structures of Alduin and others? *Skyrim* anticipates these questions and puts them on the lips of the Greybeard Arngeir in the epilogue and so implicitly (though subtly) asks the player to consider the ramifications of a witnessed eschatology. How can we wrestle with death and what manner of existence awaits us on the other side? Is moral law or responsibility realized in view of whether or what an afterlife is (that is, is eschatology transformative?), or do eschatologies function like idols, mere projections of human desires and reflections of human values, regardless of reality? After the main quest is finished, these questions remain for the player to answer -- both within and outside of the game world.

SELECTED BIBIOGRAPHY

Dronke, Ursula. *The Poetic Edda : Volume II : Mythological Poems.* Oxford: Clarendon Press, 1997.

Kelly, Anthony. *Eschatology and Hope.* Maryknoll, New York: Orbis, 2006.

Ormerod, Neil. *Creation, Grace, and Redemption.* Maryknoll, New York: Orbis, 2007.

Rahner, Karl. *On the Theology of Death,* trans. C.H. Henkey, revised by W.J. O'Hara, 2nd Edition New York: Herder and Herder, 1965.

Rahner, Karl and Karl-Heinz Weger. *Our Christian Faith: Answers for the Future.* New York: Crossroad Publishing Company, 1981.

Ratzinger, Joseph. *Eschatology: Death and Eternal Life.* 2nd Edition. Washington, D.C.: Catholic University of America Press, 1988.

Simek, Rudolf. *Dictionary of Northern Mythology,* translated by Angela Hall. Rochester, New York: D.S. Brewer, 2007.

Endnotes

[1] Joseph Ratzinger, *Eschatology: Death and Eternal Life*, Second Edition, (Washington, D.C.: Catholic University of America Press, 1988), 77.

[2] Worship of the ninth divine, Talos, is prohibited by the Empire. For more on Talos-worship, see Joshua Wise's essay on apotheosis in this volume.

[3] Ratzinger, 233.

[4] For the purpose of this article, let us bracket the question of whether Heaven, Hell, or any other modes of existence exist beyond our imaginations.

[5] This matter is taken up in a fashion by Joshua Wise in his essay on conceptual worlds, in this volume.

[6] In both Danish and Norwegian, søvn means "sleep," and gard means "dwelling," "land," or "courtyard." The modern English "garden" comes from this root also.

[7] Shor (the Nordic understanding of Lorkhan) is the god of the underworld in the Nordic pantheon. Though he is a "dead" god, he nevertheless continues to live on as ruler of Sovngarde. Tales about Shor / Lorkhan are colored heavily by cultural bias in *The Elder Scrolls*, but it is almost unanimously believed that the Mundus was created through his instigation, and that he was subsequently killed, confining his agency to the afterlife. There are some obvious

parallels with the ancient Egyptian god Osiris (a formerly living god, whose consort remains a living goddess, who now reigns over the dead in the afterlife), though a thorough treatment of these is beyond the scope of this essay.

[8] Ratzinger, 234.

[9] ...if they were not werewolves, that is. Lycanthropes, unfortunately, are claimed by Hircine, for eternal participation in the Great Hunt. Curing a Nord of lycanthropy, even posthumously, allows his or her soul to proceed to Sovngarde.

[10] From *Adversus Haereses* 4.18.5, quoted in Anthony Kelly, Eschatology and Hope, (Maryknoll, New York: Orbis, 2006), 181.

[11] Kelly, 182.

[12] *Sacrosanctum Concilium* 10.

[13] Some care has been taken to ecumenize the language here, but as the notion of Eucharistic feast is almost certainly most associated with the Catholic and Eastern Orthodox churches, language about this will default to these traditions.

[14] From *Postilla super Psalmos 33,8*, translated in Kelly, 200.

[15] John Paul II, *Ecclesia de Eucharistia 18*, quoted in Kelly, 200.

[16] ...as is covered by several other essays in this book.

[17] Karl Rahner, *On the Theology of Death,* trans. C.H. Henkey, revised by W.J. O'Hara, 2nd Edition (New York: Herder and Herder, 1965), 84.

[18] Kelly, 141.

[19] Karl Rahner and Karl-Heinz Weger, *Our Christian Faith: Answers for the Future* (New York: Crossroad Publishing Company, 1981), 119.

[20] The Soul Cairn is added to *Skyrim* in the expansion *Dawnguard*.

[21] Traditional Christian prayers for the soul(s) of the deceased include: "Eternal rest, grant unto them, O Lord and let perpetual light shine upon them. May they rest in peace. Amen." and "May her soul and the souls of all the faithful departed, through the mercy of God, rest in peace. Amen."

[22] Revelation chs 12 and 13.

[23] For more on cyclic eschatology in the Eddur, see Rudolf Simek, *Dictionary of Northern Mythology*, translated by Angela Hall (D.S. Brewer, 2007), 189, 222-224.

[24] See Joshua Wise's essay on Apotheosis in this volume.

[25] Jesus makes a similar offer regarding knowledge in the thirteenth chapter of the Gospel of Matthew, when he says to Peter, "To you it has been given to know the secrets of the kingdom of heaven, but to them it has not been given. For him who has will more be given, and he will have abundance; but from him who has not, even what he has will be taken away." While the gospel has connotations of being blessed with divine understanding, Alduin's messianic offering is about worldly dominance - again, anti-Christic.

[26] Ratzinger, 77.

[27] Ratzinger, 76.

[28] Ursula Dronke, *The Poetic Edda : Volume II : Mythological Poems*, (Oxford: Clarendon Press, 1997): 18, 124-25.

[29] Kelly, 105.

[30] Alduin was worshiped as a god in the Ancient Nordic pantheon, though his claim that he was the "first-born of Akatosh" and other distinctions made in game point not so much to his

equality in status with the Aedra, but to his unique role in the cosmos as the World-Eater, similar to the almost perpetually existent Fenrir, Jormungar, and other creatures of Norse mythology.

[31] Neil Ormerod, *Creation, Grace, and Redemption*, (Maryknoll, New York: Orbis, 2007), 85. In his notes, Ormerod reminds the reader that the content about Satan in the minds of most Christians owes more to the imaginations of the Church Fathers and subsequent poets and authors such as Dante and Milton than it does to Christian scripture.

[32] See the Book of Revelation, chs. 12-20.

[33] Scholars generally acknowledge the problem that the Eddic works were only written down after Christianity had come to Norse society. Whether or to what degree Christian mythology itself influenced those works in the form in which we have them is difficult to say, but remains a question considered by scholars (such as Rudolf Simek, among others).

[34] Kelly, 106. Janet Martin Soskice is quoted from "The Ends of Man and the Future of God," in Polkinghorne and Welker, *The End of the Word and the Ends of God*, p. 79.

[35] In addition to this, there is also the fact that while the eschatological problem is prominently engaged, it is engaged instrumentally rather than being engaged *per se.*

[36] See Mark Hayse's essay in this volume.

[37] see Jean-Luc Marion, *God without Being*, trans. Thomas A. Carlson (Chicago: University of Chicago Press, 1991), 7-24; and William Desmond, *Hegel's God: A Counterfeit Double?* (Burlington, Vermont: Ashgate, 2003), ix, and Kelly, 190.

[38] Kelly, 190.

[39] See also Matthew Frank's essay in this volume.

Dividing by Zero:
Atheism and Apologia

BY MICHAEL ZEIGLER

"The old gods are cruel and arbitrary, and distant from the hopes and fears of men. Your age is past. We are the new gods, born of the flesh, and wise and caring of the needs of our people. Spare us your threats and chiding, inconstant spirit. We are bold and fresh, and will not fear you." – Sotha Sil

Introduction

I first encountered the New Atheists in a Sunday school class. My church was doing a series about the conflict between science and faith and I was asked to moderate one of the discussions. I was given a video, some resources and was asked to facilitate a discussion. The video was of Alister McGrath pointing out the multitudinous failures of Richard Dawkins and the other New Atheists, discussing their inability to grasp either philosophy or theology. At the time, I was in seminary and had not had much time to read up on the so-called Four Horsemen, but most of what McGrath reported of Dawkins sounded like pretty standard atheist fare and I quickly returned to my contemplation of the hypostatic union.

Since then, I've come up to speed. The Four Horsemen of the New Atheists – Sam Harris, Daniel Dennet, Richard Dawkins and the late Christopher Hitchens – have been leading an all-out assault on religion – all religion – for almost a decade. Science, philosophy and verbal brutality are their weapons of choice. In response people of faith have acted in kind, with the internet becoming a wasteland of mutilated arguments, dead beliefs and skulking doubts. There are hard feelings on all sides and the battle does not look to end anytime soon. Even as both sides claim victory, new assaults are launched with accusations of child abuse, racism, sexism and intellectual dishonesty.

Apologetics is not something new. One could argue that Peter was the first apologist, standing to explain the events of Pentecost.[1] Christians have always sought to defend their faith and show that it is reasonable, just and fair. And true. As we engage with the New Atheists, their ferocity begs consideration not only of our content, but our methodology. As we do this we will look to *The Elder Scrolls* series for an example of two cultures – one religious, one atheist – and the way in which their interactions shaped both. In this way we can hope, not only to defend our faith, but to present a credible witness to a Gospel so many need to hear.

A Prologue:
OF CHIMER AND DWEMER

The first war between humans and Elves ended with the death of Lorkhan, the god who had inspired the others to create the world, and whom had been supported by humans. The Aedra Trinimac tore Lorkhan's heart from his chest and cast it far into the east, never (he believed) to be seen again. As the humans retreated to favor their wounds the Elves began to spread over the new creation, leaving their ancestral home Aldmeris (or "Old Ehlnofey"), and settling in various places. The Aldmer (the Elves of Aldmeris) became different Elven clans depending on where they settled, the most populous being the Altmer who lived on the Summerset Isles to the southwest of the continent of Tamriel.

At a time that is not commonly agreed upon by in-game historians, a group of Elves began to question the beliefs of the Altmer. The exact nature of the initial disagreement is not known, but appears to deal with Aldmeri ancestor worship and the sundering of the Elves from the Divine. In Altmeri versions of the creation story, Lorkhan deceived the gods into creating the world, an act which led to their deaths, and the sundering of their children (the Elves) from the immortal realm of Aetherius. Commenting on Aldmeri ancestor worship, Vivec, the Dunmeri God-King of Morrowind, said,

> "[W]e concern ourselves with intensity and its relationship with action, valorizing 'little narratives' and proliferation of narratives in our native cultures to the point that there is no perch from extraneous content. Pure subjectivity is no longer possible; instead it becomes akin to sensory deprivation, yet without the fear, for we sense things *that remind us of the dawn*...the quest toward *the ur-you* for certainty and foundations is not innocent. However, it is an honest vindication for truth and superhuman ideals, which means it should be regarded as such by our own sense of fault: we made this, we dreamed this, we made it viable by voting with our seductions, we will live again to show our genuine applause." (emphasis mine)[2]

Vivec, as ever, is difficult to understand. In very basic terms, Aldmeri ancestor worship is centered on a return to the Divine, that is to say an attempt to undo the sub-gradience of creation viz. the Aldmer, and restore the Elves to their status as et'Ada (immortal spirits). A viable metaphor would be that the Elves want to return to Eden and worship their ancestors as a way to do this.[3] While most of the Elves practice some form of ancestor worship it is not clear that they are all focused on this attempt to return to "the good old days." For some, it would seem, worship of ancestors is a way to seek counsel from those who have gone before.[4] The return to Aetherius appears to be a largely Altmer endeavor.[5]

Hence the divide among Elves and the Chimer exodus. A group of Altmer, led by the prophet Veloth, felt that the return to Aetherius was misguided and sought to leave the Summerset Isles and seek a home elsewhere. They were confronted by Trinimac, but the Daedra Boethia (Prince of Plots) intervened. Boethia convinced Trinimac to enter his mouth, swallowed the Aedra and spoke with his own voice against the return to Aetherius. Boethia, aided by the Daedra Mephala, taught the Velothi many things including the Psijic Endeavor[6] before defecating out Trinimac.[7] The Velothi pilgrims, now known as Chimer ("the Changed Ones"), left the Isles and eventually settled in modern-day Morrowind.[8] Chimeri religion, then, incorporated a version of ancestor worship, but also focused heavily on the worship of the three "good" Daedra: Boethia, Mephala and Azura. It is important to note that the chief reason for the Chimeri exodus from the Isles was religious in nature and that religious fervor was common among the Chimer.

When the Chimer came to Morrowind with its lava fields, swamps, grasslands and coastal islands, they were not alone. A clan of Aldmer had settled there long ago and had developed a very different ideology than any of the other Elves. These were the Dwemer, or "Deep Folk."

The early history of the Dwemer[9] is not known. While there are Dwemer ruins dotting the nations of Hammerfell, High Rock and Skyrim their principle lands seem to have been in Morrowind. How they came to those lands is a mystery; what is known is that the Dwemer culture developed in radically different ways than among other Elves. This leads many in-game scholars to suggest the Dwemer broke away from the Aldmer at a very early date. By the time Veloth and his followers arrived, the Dwemer had settled the region and built huge underground cities.

There are two things that set the Dwemer apart from other Elves. The first is their use of technology and magic. While Nordic humans were living in wooden huts and the Altmer were building cities of white stone, the Dwemer delved underground and built cities powered by geothermal energy. As the player wanders through Dwemer ruins, they find electric lights, steam engines and a multiplicity of devices of unknowable usage. In various games, one encounters airships, observatories that look out into Oblivion, and the ever-present animunculi. These steam-powered machines seem to serve a number of functions, from simple workers to guardians, and are a mystery to everyone but the Dwemer. It is not clear how they are powered or how they continue to exist, seemingly without maintenance, long after the Dwemer have disappeared. Many have come to believe that the Dwemer fused science and magic together and this is what gave them their great power.

It is the second difference that makes the Dwemer so unique: the Dwemer were staunch atheists. This may not seem so strange in our own world but one must remember that on Nirn, the gods and Daedra readily and regularly make themselves known. Boethia, Mephala and Azura aided the Chimer, but one has only to look at the other nations of Tamriel to hear stories of Shor, Yffre, the "Hoon Ding" or the other thirteen Daedric Lords; indeed the existence of vampirism in Tamriel is a direct consequence of Molag Bal's desire to spite Arkay, the Aedra of the Circle of Life and Death. The folk of Skyrim cowering at the baying of werewolves were nightly reminded of Hircine, Daedric Prince of the Hunt, and his curse upon the people of Tamriel. Despite all of this, the Dwemer denied the existence of the gods and Daedra. In the words of former Bethesda developer Michael Kirkbride, the Dwemer "knew that phenomena (that which can be perceived by the senses) and noumena (that which is the thing-itself) were both illusions, with the second one just being more clever. Dwarves could divide by zero. There isn't even a word to describe the Dwarven view on divinity. They were atheists on a world where gods exist."[10]

As might be suspected, the arrival of a new people-group looking for a land to settle did not go over well with the land's current inhabitants. It was not long before Chimer and Dwemer were in conflict. It is important to note that their conflict did not merely occur over land rights; the fervently religious Chimer were offended to the point of violence by Dwemer atheism. Were it not for the invasion of the Nords under High King Vrage, the Dwemer and Chimer may have fought a war of genocide. But the coming of the northern barbarians gave the Elves a common foe and they united to expel the invaders. In the aftermath the Dwemer and Chimer were able to set aside their differences and founded the First Council, a united body to govern the newly named Resdayn, home of both races. No small part of this alliance seems to have come from the friendship of the Dwemer King, Dumac, sometimes called Dwarf-orc, and the Chimer King, Nerevar. In the centuries to come both would be central to their people's continued alliance. Despite their differences there was peace between them for some time.[11]

THE NEW ATHEISM

People who grew up in the generation before me can tell you where they were when they heard that President Kennedy had been shot; I can tell you where I was when I heard about the 9/11 attacks. I had just dropped my wife off at work and had stopped at a local McDonald's for breakfast – I believe I was working on my (heretofore unpublished) novel between bites. I noticed some of the workers were agitated and they told me someone had crashed an airplane into the World Trade Center. In the news recently, there had been stories of harried air-traffic controllers and near misses; I could not imagine what might have caused such a horrible tragedy. It wasn't until I got home that I learned the truth: religious terrorists had purposely crashed commercial airliners into the Twin Towers. I was watching the news as they fell. And in that brief period of hours, the world changed.

There was, as one might suspect, an immediate visceral backlash against Islam. But it wasn't until 2004 that Sam Harris' *The End of Faith* turned the attack against religion itself. Harris was not alone and in 2006, Daniel Dennet's *Breaking the Spell* and Richard Dawkins' *The God Delusion* joined the assault. The following year Christopher Hitchens' *God is Not Great* completed what would come to be known as the Four Horsemen of the New Atheism. One author wrote, "The New Atheists will not let us off the hook simply because we are not doctrinaire believers. They condemn not just belief in God but respect for belief in God. Religion is not only wrong; it's evil. Now that the battle has been joined, there's no excuse for shirking."

Atheism, of course, is nothing new. What was new about the Horsemen was their backing by major publishers and their vehemence. It was the latter that made such a deep impression on religious believers.[12] Dawkins' wrote, "I am not attacking any particular version of God or gods. I am attacking God, all gods, anything and everything supernatural, wherever and whenever they have been or will be invented."[13] "Violent, irrational, intolerant," Hitchens declared of religion. "Allied to racism and tribalism and bigotry, invested in ignorance and hostile to free inquiry, contemptuous of women and coercive toward children: organized religion ought to have a great deal on its conscience."[14]

There has been an intense backlash. Author Murtaza Hussain accused Harris, and the other Horsemen, of racism, especially in their attacks on Islam. "While they attempt to couch their language in the terms of pure critique of religious thought, in practice they exhibit many of the same tendencies toward generalisation and ethno-racial condescension as did their predecessors - particularly in their descriptions of Muslims."[15] Greenwald suggested that Harris was not "a "racist," but rather that he and others like him "spout and promote Islamophobia under the guise of rational atheism." Harris did not help himself when he said, "The outrage that Muslims feel over US and British foreign policy is primarily the product of theological concerns. Devout Muslims consider it a sacrilege for infidels to depose a Muslim tyrant and occupy Muslim lands — no matter how well intentioned the infidels or malevolent the tyrant. Because of what they believe about God and the afterlife and the divine provenance of the Koran, devout Muslims tend to reflexively side with other Muslims, no matter how sociopathic their behavior."[16]

It has not been only Muslims who have critiqued the Horsemen; there have been atheist voices as well. Writing about the New Atheists' war on religion, Bryan Appleyard said, "Religion is not going to go away. It is a natural and legitimate response to the human condition, to human consciousness and to human ignorance…Furthermore, as Hitchens in effect acknowledged and as the neo-atheists demonstrate by their ideological rigidity and savagery, absence of religion does not guarantee that the demonic side of our natures will be eliminated…The history of attempts to destroy religion is littered with the corpses of believers and unbelievers alike. There are many roads to truth, but cultish intolerance is not one of them."[17] Supporters of the Horsemen have been vicious in their rebuttals. "Appleyard's article is…so deluded that it is difficult even to find an entry point for correction. It hails from a familiar genre, in which grandiose, and mostly false, assertions are made regarding the beliefs of the New Atheists…The New Atheists are lucky to have such incompetent critics."[18]

Christians, who have borne much of the Horsemen's ire (especially Dawkins'), have responded in a number of ways. Christian apologist Steven Dunn quoted Rabbi David Wolpe's response to Dawkins' Nobel Prize, "Dawkins on biology is an elegant, lucid and even enchanting explicator of science. Dawkins on religion is historically uninformed, outrageously partisan and morally obtuse. If Dawkins is indeed our best, the life of the mind is in a precarious state."[1920] A more measured response came from Dr. Douglas Groothuis of Denver Seminary when he noted the new atheists' use of straw-man arguments[21], and a failure to grasp Biblical history.[22]

But by far the most vocal critic of the Horsemen, and especially Dawkins, has been Alister McGrath. McGrath, a former atheist turned Christian, has debated several of the Horsemen, written a book called *The Dawkins Delusion?*, along with numerous articles, and spoken frequently on the subject. His tenor ranges from serious debate to somewhat-snarky repartee. In his article, "Thank God for the New Atheism," McGrath writes, "Where some seemed to think that the so-called 'Four Horsemen' would achieve final closure on the issue of God, quite the reverse seems to have happened. Cultural interest in God and religion has resurged, and the discussions are not leading to the conclusions that the New Atheism had in mind. It's a classic example of the law of unintended consequences."[23] In a lecture given at St. Edmund's Unversity McGrath systematically pointed out Dawkins' errors, concluding with a rebuttal of the Horsemen's idea that religion was the source of evil. "The real issue - as Friedrich Nietzsche pointed out over a century ago - is that there seems to be something about human nature which makes our belief systems capable of inspiring both great acts of goodness and great acts of depravity...Pretending that religion is the only problem in the world, or the base of all its pain and suffering, is simply no longer a real option for thinking people. It's just rhetoric, masking a difficult problem we all need to address - namely, how human beings can coexist and limit their passions."[24]

The observant reader will note that a great deal of the preceding paragraphs has been in-depth quotations of the critics of the New Atheists and this is by design. Whereas the Horsemen are known for the harshness of their attacks, even this brief foray into their critics reveals a similar methodology. Not all critics react with mirrored animosity, but neither are they entirely gentle. Reading the innumerable responses to the Horsemen is often like reading the recounting of a battle: volleys are fired, wounds are taken and cruelty (or at least anger) reigns. There is a defensiveness, and requisite aggression, on both sides. Christians are not immune; indeed, some of the harshest and most unforgiving of the Horsemen's opponents have been people of faith. Our *apologia* has been filled with just as much sanctimony, violence and derision as anything the Horsemen have said. Worst of all, we have most often felt justified because we are "defending the faith."

Apologetics has traditionally been defined as "the defense and explanation of the faith." There have been apologists since the moment Peter stood to explain the events of Pentecost. Whether we look to church fathers like Justin Martyr or to 20th century apologists like C.S. Lewis and Ravi Zacharias there have always been folk dedicated to the explication of the Christian message. Over the centuries, and especially since the Enlightenment, apologetics has taken on a more combative tone; one is tempted to say an intolerant tone. This has led to vicious (televised) debates, printed refutations and internet mockery. If one were not listening to the content of the discussions it would be difficult to differentiate between apologetic defense and political debate, with all of the nastiness that implies. While we need to "give a reason for the hope that is within us," there is a Scriptural need to "love our enemies and pray for those who spitefully use [us]."

A paradigm shift is needed.

The practice of peacemaking is most often thought of in terms of resolving armed conflicts, such as in the Middle East, but has been used for many years to resolve more domestic disputes as well. Neighbors angry over garbage spills, elderly grandmothers confronting teenagers who deface property, even rape victims meeting with rapists – all fall under the ministry of peacemaking. Innumerable ministries, charitable organizations and even government agencies utilize techniques meant to resolve conflict and restore harmony. Drawing principally on the work of Roger R. Nicole,[25] I hope to elucidate how altering the *way* we engage New Atheism may alter the *tenor* of our apologetic and more fully communicate the Good News of our Savior.

APOLOGETICS AS PEACEMAKING

In his article "Polemic Theology: How to Deal with Those Who Differ From Us," Nicole admits the need for Christians to "contend earnestly for the faith," to defend and explain it. He also recognizes that differences arise in interpretation, implementation and meaning – and that these differences can lead to painful, even destructive, conflict. While Nicole seemed to be writing about the church, I would like to suggest the methods he offers work in any conflict, especially apologetical quarrels. Nicole bids us ask ourselves three questions as we seek to engage with those who believe differently.

What do we owe to those different from us?

A deceptively simple question – I can hear old friends from Bible college or seminary answering, "The truth." But we owe more than this to the New Atheists. As people of God, we owe it to them to try to understand what they are saying. This is difficult. Listening to Dawkins' mock the Virgin Birth or insult Jesus is challenging to say the least. And this is part of the problem. Much of the criticism of the Horsemen is based on "soundbytes" of their works – most of us have not bothered to fully read *any* of their books. If we are going to faithfully engage with someone, we cannot base our understanding on a two-line quote – we will need to hear them speak for themselves. Reading *The God Delusion* was a painful experience for me, not only because Dawkins says hurtful (one is tempted to say vengeful) things, but because I knew that I needed to resist my own urge to lash back. Instead of reading to find his errors, I needed to read to hear his heart. Fortunately, Dawkins is pretty open with his feelings.

A theme he returns to again and again is the societal privilege of religion. "A widespread assumption, which nearly everybody in our society accepts – the non-religious included – is that religious faith is especially vulnerable to offence and should be protected by an abnormally thick wall of respect, in a different class from the respect any human being should pay to another."[26] Hence, religion is beyond criticism. Later he remarks on religious faith being built so it does not need any evidence. "Perhaps it is the very fact that there is no evidence to support theological opinions, either way, that fosters the characteristic draconian hostility towards those of slightly different opinion."[27] Taken together, these statements reveal what I feel is one of Dawkins' deepest problems with religion. He feels that, as a scientist, his views are neither wanted nor appreciated – Dawkins feels excluded from the conversation.

Another thing we owe to the New Atheists is to understand their goals. Again, I hear the internet apologist roaring, "They want to destroy religion!" I do not believe this is the case. While the above authors have interpreted Harris' "anti-Muslim animus" as racism, I think it is fair to say there may be something else at work. Here are a few "soundbytes" from the Greenwald article: "I am one of the few people I know of who has argued in print that torture may be an ethical necessity in our war on terror...We should profile Muslims, or anyone who looks like he or she could conceivably be Muslim, and we should be honest about it... The only future devout Muslims can envisage — *as Muslims* — is one in which all infidels have been converted to Islam, politically subjugated, or killed." Pretty damning stuff, it would seem. For myself, I cannot affirm or deny Harris' racism – I don't know him well enough. But it strikes me that someone supporting torture, racial profiling and who defines another as seeking only to subjugate and kill (especially when that is clearly not the case for millions of the world's Muslims) is not speaking in hatred, but fear. Those of us who sat glued to our television sets on 9/11 can remember that fear well. Harris may be a racist – but it sounds to me that he is driven by fear.

Consider as well this quote from Hitchens: "In Belfast I have seen whole streets burned out by sectarian warfare between different sects of Christianity, and interviewed people whose relatives and friends have been kidnapped and killed or tortured by rival religious death squads, often for no other reason than membership of another confession."[28] It strikes me as fascinating that so few of the Horsemen's critics have noted that both Hitchens and Dawkins are British and have grown up listening to news reports and reading newspapers on the violence in Northern

Ireland, perhaps on a daily basis. This kind of bloodshed has a different effect when it's not thousands of miles across the Atlantic Ocean. Had any of us grown up in a situation of continual religious violence (wherever and whenever it might have been), we might believe that religion was a dangerous, poisonous influence too.

What I am suggesting is that the Horsemen see religion as the root of all evil and from their perspective, I can understand why. Their goal, I believe, is to rid society of this dangerous influence and make the world a safer place. When you believe that a singular system is the reason for all the suffering in the world you will do and say nearly anything to defeat it. The vehemence, then, of the Horsemen is born of their desire for a safer, more civil society. That goal is not an objectionable one; of course, I disagree with their assessment of the problem, as do many other authors. I recognize that this point is open to criticism as it is based on a kind of "distance psychoanalysis," but I am confident in my view. Understanding what the Horsemen are really trying to accomplish should alter the way we interact with them.

What can we learn from those who differ from us?

I can hear the roar of "Nothing!" ringing in my ears as I type this. But the truth is there is much we can learn from the Horsemen. This will require humility and a willingness to ask ourselves difficult questions.

One of the common themes in atheist criticism is the recounting of the Church's crimes; converse with an atheist and it will not be long before they are bringing up the Crusades, Salem Witch trials and the KKK. In my experience, the usual response has been, "Well, they really weren't Christians. Real Christians wouldn't do that." The first of our uncomfortable questions is: could we be wrong?

Even a brief survey of Christian history will reveal a menagerie of horrors. Conversion by the sword, the Children's Crusade, the Protestant Reformation and resultant wars, people burned at the stake for translating the Bible into the common language…our history is replete with violence. The horrifying truth is that Christians in all ages have committed atrocities in the name of God; people of real, genuine faith have murdered, stolen and raped. In a way we should not be surprised. The fallenness of humanity is a central tenant of Christianity; it is reflected in our Scriptural stories. "All have sinned and fallen short of the glory of God," and this is still true of those within the Body of Christ. To deny the faith of people because of their sin is disingenuous with our theology – even Paul had his "thorn in the side." It is time we stop trying to protect ourselves and admit our sins. Christians have done monstrous things; we are only fooling ourselves. If we truly believe in repentance, it is time we practiced it.[29] The truth will set us free.[30]

Criticism is not always a negative thing and is commended to us in Scripture as a way to combat pride and erroneous thinking.[31] Nicole suggests, "We may learn from those who object that we are not communicating as we should and that they have not rightly understood what we wanted to say." That is to say that our critics act as mirrors, reflecting back what they understand us to be saying. Of course, animus and ideological distortion may be a part of that reflection, but careful exegesis of their critique can give us great insight into how well, or not, we are communicating. A painful example of this can be found in the case of Elizabeth Smart. When asked why she did not try to flee her captors, she replied that she no longer felt she had value. As a Mormon student, she had been taught the value of sexual purity and one teacher went so far as to describe individuals who were not sexually pure as "chewed pieces of gum." As a rape victim, Smart thought, "'I'm that chewed up piece of gum, nobody re-chews a piece of gum, you throw it away.' And that's how easy it is to feel like you no longer have worth, you no longer have value...Why would it even be worth screaming out? Why would it even make a difference if you are rescued? Your life still has no value."[32] Knowing ministers who have taught on sexual purity and who have used this (it must be said) disgusting metaphor, I can attest that they do not mean to devalue human life, but to emphasize the precious gift of human intimacy. And that is the *point* – the disconnect between intention and what was communicated led to a young woman seeing herself as without value. In this case, criticism of so-called "slut-shaming"[33] exposes a serious problem in communication. Whether we believe in the message about sexual purity or not, one cannot help but see the need to change our methods of teaching.

HOW DO WE COPE WITH THOSE WHO DIFFER FROM US?

Coping with those who differ from us comes down to two major questions: how do we engage in critical reflection with them (constructive), and how do we defend ourselves against their attacks (protective)? In the end, the question comes down to aggression; when Dawkins or one of the Horsemen attacks our faith, we become angry, we want to lash out and hurt them as they have hurt us. This is something that must be resisted. Using these previous techniques, we must diffuse our anger, understand our critics and respond without aggression. When we use Scripture, we must do so reverently and carefully, avoiding the common technique of "carpet-bombing" – raining Scripture after Scripture in an attempt to force our critics into submission. Instead we must listen to their questions, do our best to offer answers and be willing to confess that we may not have all the answers they are seeking. Humility speaks volumes. And in our humility, we must be willing to struggle with our critics, remembering that the progress of the soul is rarely easy. I find it best to reflect upon Christ's command to "walk a second mile," in this case, and the admonition to "bear one another's burdens."[34]

Of course, it is likely that not everyone will agree with our message. Herein lays the great opportunity of the apologist: disagreement need not destroy relationship. How we treat those who disagree with us says as much about our Gospel as all our defenses of it, perhaps more. It will be difficult. The aggression of the Horsemen and other New Atheists begs to be reciprocated. But victory over aggression "arises in the unique moment of each circumstance. It preserves the possibilities. Victory is ongoing, a way of being rather than a final goal. It means embracing all aspects of the world. Trying to reject parts of it perpetuates the struggle in oneself and in the world. Victory over war is victory over this aggression, a victory that includes the enemy and thus renders further conflict unnecessary."[35] In this case, including the Horsemen means remembering they are the beloved, if errant, children of God and in need of our common Savior. I will expand on this below.

How do we protect ourselves? The Horsemen attack with arguments we find difficult to defend against and herein is the answer – we must admit that we do not *have* all the answers. Apologetics is a process of discerning truth (and Truth) and is transformative; it requires time. We will need the whole Body of Christ for support, knowledge and refining. Whether it is the encouragement of our local church, the writings of Church Fathers (and Mothers), or the empowering of the Holy Spirit found in prayer, meditation upon the Word, or in the sacral experience of doubt – the apologist must remember they are not alone. The "great cloud of witnesses" stands behind us, God sustains us.

But the greatest armor, the best weapon, the most profound comfort comes from joy. Life is more than finding answers and defending them – though that is a kind of joy itself. All of creation is a gift and Christ has called us to love and be loved. We can draw strength from the generosity of the Creator, the fellowship of friends and family and the simple joy of living. Sometimes the best apologists leave their keyboards and go for a walk. Or play video games. And through the joy of the Lord, we come fresh to our critics and, one hopes, respond in love.

In dealing with those who differ from us, even those who hate us, it is well to reflect on Nicole's words. "Perhaps the most important consideration for the Christian is to remain aware at all times of the goal to be achieved. It is the consistent perception of this goal that will give a basic orientation to the whole discussion: Are we attempting to win an argument in order to manifest our own superior knowledge and debating ability? Or are we seeking to win another person whom we perceive as enmeshed in error or inadequacy by exposing him or her to the truth and light that God has given to us?" The purpose of apologetics is not to prove or disprove, but to reveal the love of God.

THE BATTLE OF RED MOUNTAIN

But by this point, many readers will be wondering what any of this has to do with *The Elder Scrolls* and its Elven peoples. In our prologue, we considered the tale of the passionately religious Chimer and devoutly atheistic Dwemer. The two peoples united against a common enemy despite their differences. But their newfound unity was not to last.[36]

Together the Dwemer and Chimer had driven the Nords and their Orc mercenaries from the land. In the years that followed, they forged a new realm – Resdayn; the realm and its peace were, in no small way, inspired by the friendship of their Kings, Nerevar and Dumac. Despite the concerns of Nerevar's Tribunal of councilors (Vivec, Sotha Sil and his queen Almalexia), the Dwemer and Chimer lived in relative harmony for centuries.

Then Dagoth Ur, head of the Chimer House Dagoth and friend to both Dumac and Nerevar, came to the Chimer King with proof that the Dwemer had found the Heart of Lorkhan and were using it in some profane way, "tap[ping] its powers, and…building a new god, a mockery of Chimer faith and a fearsome weapon." Though the Tribunal counseled war, Nerevar went to his friend to learn if the rumor was true. But Kagrenac, greatest of the Dwemer engineers (or "Tonal Architects") took offense at the Chimer King's questions and asked what right he had to interfere or judge the Dwemer.

Nerevar, deeply troubled, made pilgrimage to the temple of Azura and there sought the Daedra's wisdom. She told him that Dagoth Ur had spoken truly and the new Dwemer god must be stopped at any cost. Upon hearing her pronouncement, the Tribunal again counseled war and again Nerevar sought his friend Dumac. They quarreled bitterly and when next Nerevar came, he came with an army.

The Battle of Red Mountain would be remembered for generations. Through cunning the Chimer drew the armies of the Dwemer out of their mountain fastness and a small band of warriors led by Nerevar and Dagoth Ur entered the Dwemer citadel. There the two friends met again with swords and Dumac fell to the Chimer King, though Nerevar was grievously wounded. Kagrenac, seeing defeat was at hand, turned his tools upon the Heart of Lorkhan…and the Dwemer, everywhere and all at once, vanished and were never seen again.

Dagoth Ur came to Nerevar for the tools of Kagrenac remained. "That fool Kagrenac has destroyed his own people with these things," he said. "We should destroy them, right away, lest they fall into the wrong hands."

But Nerevar doubted himself and resolved to speak to the Tribunal, for their advice about the Dwemer had been right and his love for his friend wrong. He commanded Dagoth Ur to hold the tools in trust while he was taken from the citadel to confer with his counselors.

Here the narrative becomes confused and many versions differ. There is no doubt that the Tribunal advised keeping the tools and that Nerevar required them all to swear an oath to Azura never to use them. Together Nerevar and the Tribunal returned to the citadel and there Dagoth Ur refused to give up the tools. Vivec would later suggest Dagoth had already learned the use of the tools and may have begun using them to attain immortality. Battle ensued. In some versions Nerevar died of his wounds, in some he survived to return to the Chimer capital. In all, Dagoth Ur was defeated and the tools recovered. They were given to Sotha Sil who studied their magical properties.

It is not clear when the Tribunal betrayed Nerevar. In some versions, they killed him during their oath to Azura, in others he fell fighting Dagoth Ur and in others he was slain at the capital. What is clear is that Vivec, Sotha Sil and Almalexia betrayed their King and used the tool to attain the power of gods.

Millennia later, Vivec would recall:

> "And no sooner than we had completed our rituals and begun to discover our new-found powers, the Daedra Lord Azura appeared and cursed us for our foresworn oaths. By her powers of prophecy, she assured us that her champion, Nerevar, true to his oath, would return to punish us for our perfidy, and to make sure such profane knowledge might never again be used to mock and defy the will of the gods. But Sotha Sil said to her, 'The old gods are cruel and arbitrary, and distant from the hopes

and fears of mer. Your age is past. We are the new gods, born of the flesh, and wise and caring of the needs of our people. Spare us your threats and chiding, inconstant spirit. We are bold and fresh, and will not fear you.'"

In that moment, the Chimer became Dunmer; their skin lost its golden hue and turned ashen and gray, their eyes became red like fire. The Tribunal were frightened at first, but Sotha Sil's encouraging words gave them heart and they emerged to lead their new people. Over time, they built great cities, bore great institutions and Resdayn knew unbroken peace and prosperity. But beneath Red Mountain, Dagoth Ur slumbered, drawing darkness to himself. In time, the tools of Kagrenac were lost and Dagoth Ur harnessed the power of the Heart, crafting a new race of Ash monsters, diseases and a new god. The power of the Tribunal waned and over them hung always the threat of Azura – her champion Nerevar would come again and right their wrongs, and punish them for their sins.

Outraged by the blasphemy of the Dwemer and with the death of Nerevar and Dumac's friendship, a war occurred that devastated the nation of Resdayn. It is not clear what happened to the Dwemer; some claim they achieved a kind of immortality, others that they were all killed. What is clear is that the Dwemer were gone and the Chimer forever changed. In victory, they transformed themselves into the Dunmer and as Azura said "all is darkness." By the time the Nerevarine comes, Morrowind is in turmoil, is in the midst of violent religious upheaval and the Tribunal no longer walks among their people. Vivec is weary, Almalexia has gone mad and Sotha Sil is grateful for the death that takes him.

In the words of Nietzsche, "He who does battle with monsters needs to watch out lest he in the process become a monster himself." The New Atheists are not monsters; but if we give in to our aggression, we may find ourselves walking the path of the Tribunal.

CONCLUSION

The New Atheism affords the Church a profound opportunity. In the last century, Christianity has endured a tremendous number of attacks: political, social, theological, scientific. As we have struggled to survive these assaults we have relied upon old adages, thrown out sections of Scripture or closed our ears. By entering into dialogue with our critics, we allow ourselves to see ourselves in a new light – to see through a different lens. But we also allow our critics to see us in a new light as well. If we can transcend the need to strike back, if we can let love – not the desire for victory – lead us, if we can find a way to include rather than exclude those who would destroy religion, we may say more about our Savior that we have said in a long, long time.

The problem is not debate. The Christian church has a long, fruitful history of theological discussion; the problem comes when that debate becomes violent, verbally or otherwise. Wars have been fought over clauses in creeds, whole cities left to be ransacked because of a difference in Christology. At its heart, our greatest challenge is to change the way we view conflict. If our critics are viewed as enemies to be destroyed, there will be horror and death before the end – perhaps literally. But if we view our critics, and the resultant conflict, as an avenue for change, adaptation – as a new way to reach out to others – we will transform the very nature of that conflict. We are still going to disagree; I very much doubt this article would cause Richard Dawkins to fall on his knees and confess Christ as Savior. But it may give us a way to make him doubt.

"A young man who wishes to remain a sound Atheist," wrote C.S. Lewis, "cannot be too careful of his reading. There are traps everywhere— 'Bibles laid open, millions of surprises,' as Herbert says, 'fine nets and stratagems.' God is, if I may say it, very unscrupulous."[37] God is always seeking to reach those who reject Him; always seeking the lost coin, the lost child, the lost sheep. God speaks in ways we might never expect and our arguments are only a small part of the Sprit's work. Let us remember why we speak; let us remember our great commission. Let us remember that we too once rebelled against God and that it was His love that called us home.

WORKS CITED

Dawkins, Richard. *The God Delusion*. Houghton Mifflin Company: Boston, 2006.

Hitchens, Christopher. *God is Not Great*. Twelve: New York, 2007.

Lewis, C.S. *Surprised by Joy*. Harcourt Brace and Company: San Diego, 1955.

"Sage Commander, The." *The Art of War*. Shambhala: Boston, 2001.

ONLINE WORKS CITED

Appleyard, Bryan. *The God Wars*. *http://www.newstatesman.com/ religion/2012/02/neo-atheism-atheists-dawkins*. Retrieved 6/24/2013.

Battle of Red Mountain, The.http://www.imperial-library.info/content/ battle-red-mountain. Retrieved 6/23/2013.

Before the Ages of Man.http://www.uesp.net/wiki/Lore:Before_the_ Ages_of_Man. Retrieved 6/23/2013.

Culp-Ressler, Tara. *Elizabeth Smart: Abstinence Education Teaches Rape Victims They're Worthless, Dirty, And Filthy*. *http://thinkprogress.org/ health/2013/05/06/1967591/elizabeth-smart-abstinence-ed/?mobile=nc* Retrieved 6/27/2013.

Definitive Guide to the Dwemer. *http://www.imperial-library.info/content/definitive-guide-dwemer#10.* Retrieved 6/23/2013.

Doors of the Spirit.http://www.imperial-library.info/content/doorsspirit. Retrieved 6/24/2013.

Dunn, Steven. *What Shall We Make of Richard Dawkins? http://www.christianapologeticsalliance.com/2013/05/21/what-shall-we-make-of-richard-dawkin/.* Retrieved 6/24/2013.

Dwarves.http://norse-mythology.org/gods-and-creatures/dwarves/ Retrieved 7/19/2013.

FAQ: What is Slut-Shaming? http://finallyfeminism101.wordpress.com/2010/04/04/what-is-slut-shaming/. Retrieved 7/19/2013.

Flynn, Tom. *Why I Don't Believe in the New Atheism. http://www.secularhumanism.org/index.php?section=library&page=flynn_30_3.* Retrieved 6/24/2013.

Greenwald, Glenn. *Sam Harris, the New Atheists, and anti-Muslim Animus. http://www.guardian.co.uk/commentisfree/2013/apr/03/sam-harris-muslim-animus.* Retrieved 6/25/2013.

Groothuis, Douglas. *Understanding the New Atheism, Part 1: The Straw God. http://www.denverseminary.edu/understanding-the-new-atheism-part-1-the-straw-god/.* Retrieved 6/24/2013.

Groothuis, Douglas. *Understanding the New Atheism, Part 2: Attacks on the New Testament. http://www.denverseminary.edu/understanding-the-new-atheism-part-1-the-straw-god/.* Retrieved 6/24/2013.

Hussain, Murtaza. *Scientific racism, militarism, and the new atheists. http://www.aljazeera.com/indepth/opinion/2013/04/20134210413618256.html.* Retrieved 6/24/2013.

Lore: Chimer. http://www.uesp.net/wiki/Lore:Chimer Retrieved 6/23/2013.

Lore: Dwemer. http://www.uesp.net/wiki/Lore:Dwemer Retrieved 6/24/2013.

McGrath, Alister. *Has Science Eliminated God? Richard Dawkins and the Meaning Of Life.http://www.st-edmunds.cam.ac.uk/CIS/mcgrath/lecture.html.* Retrieved 6/24/2013.

McGrath, Alister. *Thank God for the New Atheism. http://www.abc.net.au/religion/articles/2011/01/31/3125641.htm.* Retrieved 6/24/2013.

Nerevar at Red Mountain.http://www.imperial-library.info/content/nerevar-red-mountain. Retrieved 6/24/2013.

Nicole, Roger R. *Polemic Theology: How to Deal With Those Who Differ From Us. http://www.founders.org/journal/fj33/article3.html* Retrieved 6/24/2013.

Poirier, Alfred J. *The Cross and Criticism. http://www.peacemaker.net/site/apps/nlnet/content3.aspx?c=aqKFLTOBlpH&b=1084263&ct=1245843&notoc=1.* Retrieved 6/24/2013.

Pocket Guide to the Empire, 3rd Edition. http://www.uesp.net/wiki/Lore:Pocket_Guide_to_the_Empire,_3rd_Edition. Retrieved 6/23/2013.

Rosenhouse, Jason. *New Atheism's Critics Need to Suck it Up. http://scienceblogs.com/evolutionblog/2012/03/09/new-atheisms-critics-need-to-s/.* Retrieved 6/24/2013.

Wolpe, David. *Is Richard Dawkins Really the World's Leading Intellectual? http://www.huffingtonpost.com/rabbi-david-wolpe/is-richard-dawkins-really-the-worlds-leading-intellectual_b_3226638.html.* Retrieved 7/19/2013.

Valentinian View of the Creation, The. http://www.gnosis.org/library/valentinus/Valentinian_Creation.htm. Retrieved on 7/19/2013.

Vehk's Teachings.http://www.imperial-library.info/content/vehks-teaching. Retrieved 4-13-2013.

Endnotes

[1] Of course certain Old Testament prophets might be considered apologists as well. Jonah, Nahum, and Obadiah, among others, could all be considered apologists or evangelists in their ministries.

[2] *http://www.imperial-library.info/content/vehks-teaching*

[3] One can also see a parallel with the Valentinian desire to be freed from the flesh. See *http://www.gnosis.org/library/valentinus/Valentinian_Creation.htm*

[4] *http://www.imperial-library.info/content/doors-spirit*

[5] *http://www.uesp.net/wiki/Lore:Before_the_Ages_of_Man;* see also **http://www.uesp.net/wiki/Lore:Pocket_Guide_to_the_Empire,_3rd_Edition;** it seems that not all Altmer shared this view of mythic re-gradience and that the Psijic Order was born out of Altmeri rejection of this idea. It is not clear if the Order maintains this view. What does seem clear is that the Thalmor of the 4th Era have made it the core ideology of their pogroms.

[6] Or the pursuit of CHIM. For a more complete consideration of CHIM and the Amaranth see my article "The Heart of the World" in this volume.

[7] Trinimac, transformed in the bowels of Boethia, became the Daedra Malacath and his followers became the Orcs. For further information see *http://www.uesp.net/wiki/Lore:Chimer*

[8] Or Dwemereth. The lands surrounding Red Mountain have undergone numerous changes of name throughout history. Morrowind is the current name of the region.

[9] Any discussion of the Dwemer must begin with their name. The Aldmeris **Dwemer** means "deep elves", "deep folk" or "people of the deep", but the Dwemer are more commonly known as Dwarves. This has led to the misconception that short men with beards were found by the Chimer mining for gold and crafting exquisitely beautiful works. This is simply not the case; there are no Tolkien dwarves in The Elder Scrolls series (alas). The misnomer "dwarf" is believed to have been given to the Dwemer by a race of giants that once populated Morrowind, or perhaps by the giants of Skyrim who encountered them during their travels. Though Dwemer men often sported beards they seem to have been of roughly human height. For further information see *http://www.uesp.net/wiki/Lore:Dwemer* It is also worth noting the similarities between the Dwemer and the dvergr, or dwarves, of Norse mythology. Both were skilled in creating powerful and beautiful objects (not the least of which included Thor's hammer Mjollnir), lived underground and were not necessarily of shorter stature. In a fascinating twist the Dwarves of Norse myth are sometimes called Dark Elves (Old Norse *svartálfar)*. For further information see *http://norse-mythology.org/gods-and-creatures/dwarves/*

[10] *http://www.imperial-library.info/content/definitive-guide-dwemer#10*

[11] *http://www.uesp.net/wiki/Lore:Dwemer*

[12] Flynn *http://www.secularhumanism.org/index.php?section=library&page=flynn_30_3*

[13] Dawkins 36

[14] Hitchens 56

[15] *http://www.aljazeera.com/indepth/opinion/2013/04/20134210413618256.html*

[16] Quoted in - *http://www.guardian.co.uk/commentisfree/2013/apr/03/sam-harris-muslim-animus*

[17] *http://www.newstatesman.com/religion/2012/02/neo-atheism-atheists-dawkins*

[18] *http://scienceblogs.com/evolutionblog/2012/03/09/new-atheisms-critics-need-to-s/*

[19] *http://www.christianapologeticsalliance.com/2013/05/21/what-shall-we-make-of-richard-dawkin/*

[20] See also Wolpe's article on Huffington Post, *http://www.huffingtonpost.com/rabbi-david-wolpe/is-richard-dawkins-really-the-worlds-leading-intellectual_b_3226638.html*

[21] Groothuis *http://www.denverseminary.edu/understanding-the-new-atheism-part-1-the-straw-god/*

[22] Groothuis *http://www.denverseminary.edu/understanding-the-new-atheism-part-2-attacks-on-the-new-testament/*

[23] *http://www.abc.net.au/religion/articles/2011/01/31/3125641.htm*

[24] McGrath *http://www.st-edmunds.cam.ac.uk/CIS/mcgrath/lecture.html*

[25] Nicole *http://www.founders.org/journal/fj33/article3.html*

[26] Dawkins 20

[27] Dawkins 34

[28] Hitchens 18

[29] Working out why Christians have done these things is an entirely other consideration. Whether Christianity has been corrupted by political power or sexual repression is a subject that must be addressed by another author.

[30] Of course this raises the deeper question about the Bible, tradition, and doctrine; the Horsemen are not simply attacking the Church's *actions*, but the very core of its *beliefs*. In this at least, the Christian has little to worry about. For the Horsemen, "New" though they be, are saying nothing that has not been said before. These arguments have been going on for thousands of years and the greatest minds have been pondering them all that time. Christianity has weathered critics and skeptics before, and very often found them joining the fold.

[31] Poirier *http://www.peacemaker.net/site/apps/nlnet/content3.aspx?c=aqKFLTOBlpH&b=1084263&ct=1245843&notoc=1*

[32] Culp-Ressler *http://thinkprogress.org/health/2013/05/06/1967591/elizabeth-smart-abstinence-ed/?mobile=nc*

[33] The Finally Feminism blog gives an excellent definition of this phenomenon. "Slut-shaming, also known as slut-bashing, is the idea of shaming and/or attacking a woman or a girl for being sexual, having one or more sexual partners, acknowledging sexual feelings, and/or acting on sexual feelings." For further information see *http://finallyfeminism101.wordpress.com/2010/04/04/what-is-slut-shaming/*

[34] Matthew 5:41 and Galatians 6:2.

[35] "The Sage Commander" 106

[36] The proceeding text is based on the in-game book, "The Battle of Red Mountain". Numerous accounts of the battle exist; this one is told by Vivec himself. *http://www.imperial-library.info/content/nerevar-red-mountain*

[37] *http://www.epubbud.com/read.php?g=9RTP6VKJ&p=14*

THE HEART OF THE WORLD:
How Creation Stories Define
Our Relationship to the Divine

BY MICHAEL ZEIGLER

INTRODUCTION

There is a special power in beginnings. When I step out the door of my home, prepared to take a walk, I look up and down my street and am presented with innumerable choices – where to go, what pace to set, what destination(s). Before I take my first step literally the whole world is ahead of me. But once I take that first step, I find myself pulling away from those myriad choices and following a singular path – down this street, past these houses. Already my mind is disconnecting. The path is predictable; I've seen these houses, that tree, that park before. I've taken only a few steps and already I'm thinking of my chair at home.

Creation stories are beginnings and they too have a special power. When we frame the first interactions of God with the earth, animals and humanity we are setting the course of how we interpret what interactions follow. If we are spirits cursed to live in flesh then flesh will be a curse. If God commands and judges then God is to be obeyed and, perhaps, feared. Out of these stories grow narratives, themes, theologies. Our praxis flows from our first vision of God.

Christianity is having a bit of a problem with its creation story. Since the emergence of Darwinian evolution, many Christians have been looking at Moses' tale of a six-day creation with embarrassment. The language is poetical, the language is literal…the arguments spin round and round. And while some scholars, especially Feminist scholars, have been looking at those early chapters of Genesis in different ways, our real problem with it isn't evolution, but how we've understood what those chapters are saying about God, the earth, animals and humanity. Our greatest struggle is with our first vision of God.

Those of us who are fans (super-fans?) of *The Elder Scrolls* video game series have noticed the power of creation stories on Nirn as well. There are many of them. And while the first visions of Tamrielic gods are different – world-serpents eating themselves, quasi-Gnostic elves, duty-driven Imperials – there is a meta-narrative that runs through them all. It is this narrative that defines the way the people of Nirn view themselves, their relationships with others, their relationships to the gods. It is the core impetus of the series; it defines everything that happens afterwards.

How we understand creation stories defines how we understand God and our relationship to God. How we handle these first narratives determines how we will handle all the narratives that follow. Because of this the way we study creation stories must be more nuanced, imaginative and open than anywhere else. Everything depends on it.[1]

THE MONOMYTH

One of the great joys (and troubles) of studying the lore of *The Elder Scrolls* is that it often disagrees with itself. The in-game books, which are an important source of lore, emulate real-world disparity and frequently contradict one another, offering a multiplicity of views. The players are left to decide for themselves (or not) what they think is true. Nowhere is this more evident than with the creation story.

A number of in-game texts deal with the creation of the Mundus but the most comprehensive – and thereby contradictory – is *The Mono-myth*.[2] Compiling creation stories from the various Tamrielic cultures the author admits the disagreement between the various myths, but points out that there are themes present in all the stories, and from this derives that the various cultures are telling a single story (monomyth) through different perspectives. There is, the author suggests, a true story that can be uncovered; how the story is interpreted by Tamriel's diverse cultures accounts for the differing myths.

What most creation stories agree on is that, before time began, there existed The One, or All, often called Anu. Anu represents stasis, or perfection in many myths. In the Yokudan myths, Anu's analog Satak is "the hum…a force so prevalent as to be not really there at all." If one can imagine the real-world god of the Greek philosophers – ineffable, perfect, unmovable - one will come close to understanding Anu. In order to better understand his own perfection, Anu created his Other (or Opposite): Padomay – Change, Imperfection, Action. Out of their interactions were born the et'Ada, or original spirits.

The existence of the et'Ada is, in many texts, described as ephemeral. It is not until Time itself emerges that the original spirits really begin to understand themselves as beings with a past, present and future. Time is often seen as the et'Ada known variously as Akatosh, Auriel or Satakal. In all myths he is a Dragon god. Once time began the spirits began to move towards a pattern of stasis: identities were established, lives were lived and the ephemeral nature of creation gave way to stability. Padomay was not pleased.

In an effort to return creation to a more chaotic (or at least less static) nature, Padomay created Lorkhan, the most controversial figure in all of *The Elder Scrolls'* lore. Lorkhan (also known as Sep, Shezzar and the Missing God) approached the other et'Ada with a grand vision. Even as Anu and Padomay had created them, so they, too, would create. Many of the et'Ada joined with Lorkhan[3] and sacrificed much of their power to create Nirn, the world.

But the sacrifice was steep. Many of the spirits, bereft of power, began to die. Some were able to escape the new creation and return to the heavens, others became "the Earth Bones" to stabilize the new world so it would not die. Some of the spirits married and had children as a way to live on; each generation became weaker and weaker until even the strongest (the elves) were bound to mortality and death. The et'Ada who had aided Lorkhan (later called the Aedra, or "our ancestors") were divided; many saw him as a betrayer, others as a liberator who gave them a new way to live. It was not long before there was war on Nirn. The elves, led by Akatosh, fought against Lorkhan and his human followers. Various myths suggest the world was severely damaged, entire continents sunk beneath the waves of the oceans. In the end, Lorkhan fell, killed when the knight Trinimac tore his heart from his chest. Humans carried away the body of Lorkhan and humans and elves have been in conflict ever since.

Astute readers will note that the TES creation stories pay homage to numerous mythologies and religions; the elven myth is almost Gnostic in quality.[4] But what should be clear is the meta-narrative of the entire cycle: everything comes back to Stasis and Change. Stasis is usually viewed as desirable and Change as corruption, an enemy. Even Padomay, who is Change incarnate, does not like the Change brought by Time/Akatosh (the shift from impermanence to more-permanent) and attempts to reestablish the old order of things. It is a theme that appears in most of the TES games, a meta-conflict that defines not only the relationships between the original spirits, but also among people and the gods.[5] In the world of *The Elder Scrolls* the very fabric of the universe is defined by Stasis and Change and their eternal conflict.

A GARDEN OF CHOICES

Over the last century, there has been considerable debate about the Judeo-Christian creation story, whether arguments about literality, gender-roles or that the story should simply be seen as poetry. One of the strangest things about the first chapters of Genesis is that we are never told *why* God created the universe, only that God did. Traditional thought believed that God created the universe as a way to express the Divine glory; this is seen particularly in the way creation carries out God's will. "The inanimate creation does so mechanically, obeying natural laws which govern the physical world. The animate creation does so instinctively, responding to impulses within. Man alone is capable of obeying God consciously and willingly and thus glorifies God most fully."[6] This focus on obedience and, thereby, authority likely comes from the majority of God's statements in the early chapters of Genesis being commands.[7] But it is the command given to the first humans that most often gets attention: "but of the tree of the knowledge of good and evil you shall not eat, for in the day that you eat of it you shall die."[8]

It is this commandment that sets the stage for the entirety of the Biblical drama. The first humans, like their descendents, would not obey the Divine fiat. Through their rebellion the creation was cursed, their relationships with each other and God were broken and they were cast from paradise. Outside of the garden, the rebellion of humanity only gained strength until "The LORD saw that the wickedness of humankind was great in the earth, and that every inclination of the thoughts of their hearts was only evil continually. And the LORD was sorry that he had made humankind on the earth, and it grieved him to his heart."[9] Later, God would give a Divine law to God's people, Israel, but the people, more often than not, refused to listen. One can almost hear the despair when the author of Ecclesiastes writes, "The end of the matter; all has been heard. Fear God, and keep his commandments, for that is the whole duty of everyone. For God will bring every deed into judgment, including every secret thing, whether good or evil."[10] It should be clear by this point that scripture has frequently been interpreted in terms of a meta-narrative of Authority and Obedience. Like the eternal conflict of Stasis and Change that births the world of Nirn and defines the lives of its people, so the conflict of humans and Divine authority defines human existence. In both narratives, Conflict is the protonym of the universe.

Hence, the way we understood the creation account determined the way we understand everything that follows it. Scholars have attempted to redefine the Divine-human relationship through most of the Twentieth Century but Modernist and scientific emphases have led to dismissing the creation account as poetry, mythology or misinformed ancient science; and thereby miss the origins of the conflict. Whether Scripture is viewed through the lenses of process, liberation or mystical theology, in the end, we are haunted by "fear God and keep his commandments." While many modern-day authors[11] object to the violence of Israel's sacrificial system and its fulfillment in the substitutionary theory of the atonement – where Christ accepts the punishment for human disobedience – there can be few other possibilities when the creation story is viewed in this light, as authority and obedience. Divine justice requires punishment for defiance.[12]

LORKHAN AND THE OBSCURE TEXTS

As one reads The Monomyth with its myriad views on the creation, one finds a curious statement in the Altmeri myth, *"The Heart of the World."* Lorkhan had been defeated by Trinimac but, "when Trinimac and Auriel[13] tried to destroy the Heart of Lorkhan it laughed at them. It said, 'This Heart is the heart of the world, for one was made to satisfy the other.'"

This places a rather different perspective on Lorkhan's motivation to create the world. In many of Tamriel's mythologies, Lorkhan is viewed as fulfilling the will of Padomay, which is to distort the Anuic Stasis. From the in-game book *Sithis*,[14] Padomay "sundered the nothing and mutated the parts, fashioning from them a myriad of possibilities. These ideas ebbed and flowed and faded away and this is how it should have been." When Akatosh formed and the universe became more stable, thus reflecting Anu, Padomay "begat Lorkhan and sent him to destroy the universe." But the words of the Heart of Lorkhan suggest that Lorkhan did not intend to destroy the universe or even to induce a Padomaic Change on the Anuic Stasis. Lorkhan was seeking the satisfaction of a desire, a desire somehow fulfilled in the creation of the world. The Cyrodiilic myth, *Shezzar's Song*, recounts some of what Lorkhan said to move the Aedra and it is striking. "This was a new thing that Shezarr described to the Gods, becoming mothers and fathers, being responsible, and making great sacrifices, with no guarantee of success, but Shezarr spoke beautifully to them, and moved them beyond mystery and tears."[15] While one could argue that Lorkhan was only trying to deceive the Aedra, the words of his Heart suggest otherwise. But as we have mentioned previously the in-game books are contradictory and finding a solid answer to this question cannot be found within the games themselves. To discover Lorkhan's motivations one must look to the Obscure Texts.

The Obscure Texts are a growing body of work written by game developers, long-time fans and even former employees of Bethesda Game Studios. They range from playful to mind-numbingly complex. Sometimes they elucidate the fates of characters from previous games or offer commentary on the more esoteric aspects of *The Elder Scrolls'* lore.[16] One of these latter pieces is *Vehk's Teachings*, a compilation of lessons by the mortal-become-god Vivec, written by former developer Michael Kirkbride. Fans of the game *Morrowind* will remember Vivec as the author of *The Thirty-Six Lessons of Vivec*, a complex blend of story, mysticism and metaphysical philosophy. Vivec is a character nearly as controversial as Lorkhan and many theories exist about the extent of his knowledge.[17] In *Vehk's Teachings*, the god-king offers insight into Lorkhan's motivations.

"Anu's firstborn, for he mostly desired order, was time, anon Akatosh. Padhome's[18] firstborn went wandering from the start, changing as he went, and wanted no name but was branded with Lorkhan. As time allowed more and more patterns to individualize, Lorkhan watched the Aurbis[19] shape itself and grew equally delighted and tired with each new shaping. As the gods and demons of the Aurbis erupted, the get of Padhome tried to leave it all behind for he wanted all of it and none of it all at once. It was then that he came to the border of the Aurbis.

"He saw the Tower, for a circle turned sideways is an 'I'. This was the first word of Lorkhan and he would never, ever forget it."

In The Elder Scrolls' cosmology, the universe (Aurbis) exists in the shape of a circle or wheel.[20] According to Vivec, Lorkhan saw the creation "turned sideways" and beheld the Tower, which is "I"; this changed him forever. Understanding why this experience was so important will require delving into one of the more esoteric areas of lore – CHIM and Amaranth.

Vivec described the Tower as, "How to permanently exist beyond duplexity, antithesis, or trouble. This is not an easy concept, I know. Imagine being able to feel with all of your senses the relentless alien terror that is God and your place in it, which is everywhere and therefore nowhere, and realizing that it means the total dissolution of your individuality into boundless being. Imagine that and then still being able to say 'I'. The 'I' is the Tower."[21]

"The relentless alien terror that is God" will no doubt strike the reader as a curious phrase coming from one of Tamriel's deities. Even more so when realizing one's place in God "means the total dissolution of your individuality." It is important to note that when Vivec speaks of God, he is not speaking of himself or any of Tamriel's deities, but of the Godhead. Hinted at in the Thirty-Six Lessons and Mankar Camoran's Commentaries on the Mysterium Xarxes, the Godhead is a subject of some debate among TES fans. In the briefest of terms, it is the suggestion that all of the Aurbis is the dream of a Godhead who may wake at any time. The realization that we are dreams causes the individual to "zero-sum" or lose their individuality. While some authors have suggested that the Godhead could be a fourth-wall breaking nod to the game's developers,[22] there is no reason to think it could not be an in-game reality.

CHIM, then, is "being able to feel with all of your senses the relentless alien terror that is God and your place in it…and then still being able to say 'I.'" To realize you are a dream in the imagination of a sleeping Godhead and yet maintain your Self is to achieve CHIM. Or as was once said in The Song of Pelinal, "the dream no longer requires the dreamer." Says Vivec, "[CHIM] is a return to the first brush of Anu-Padomay, where stasis and change created possibility…[it] provides an escape from all known laws of the divine worlds and the corruptions of the black sea of Oblivion" (emphasis mine). Though there is no doubt some disagreement among lore experts, it seems highly likely that Lorkhan saw (or even achieved) the possibility of CHIM and it changed him forever.

The Amaranth, then, is what comes after achieving CHIM. Jubal-lun-Sul, in-world author of the Loveletter from the Fifth Era, says, "Those who do not fail become the New Men: an individual beyond all AE, unerased and all-being. Jumping beyond the last bridge of all existence is the Last Existence, The Eternal I.

"I AM.

"A whole World of You.

"God.

"God outside of all else but his own free consciousness, hallucinating for eternity and falling into love: I AM AND I ARE ALL WE."[23] Those who achieve Amaranth transcend the Dream and become a Dreamer, dreaming their own dreams that themselves become Dreamers of new Dreams. "The New Man becomes God becomes Amaranth, everlasting hypnogogic. Hallucinations become lucid under His eye and therefore, like all parents of their children, the Amaranth cherishes and adores all that is come from Him."

Lorkhan, in seeing the Tower, saw the limitations of Stasis and Change with its conflict and desired more – finding it in transcending the creation and dreaming a new dream. Achieving this vision was another matter. Most of the texts agree that Lorkhan attempted CHIM, or perhaps Amaranth, through the creation of Nirn and failed. Vivec seems certain Lorkhan did this on purpose. "Why would Lorkhan and his (unwitting?) agents sabotage their experiments with the Tower? Why would he crumble that which he esteems?

"Perhaps he failed so you might know how not to."

Lorkhan failed to achieve his vision of a new dream so that those who followed after him might not. He sacrificed his attempt at bliss so that we might not have to. Lorkhan, then, is not a betrayer or even a savior, but a bodhisattva, one who forgoes enlightenment so that others may reach it.[24]

Viewing the TES creation story through the Obscure Texts changes the entire tenor of the world. Rather than being an endless story of conflict, violence and tension, the world of Nirn exists so that we might learn to love: "becoming mothers and fathers, being responsible, and making great sacrifices, with no guarantee of success." For those willing to break the fourth wall, *The Elder Scrolls* series become the Dream that we as players enter so that we might dream our own Dreams. It may be going too far to suggest the developers at Bethesda Game Studios created *The Elder Scrolls* to inspire others to dream new worlds, new stories. But as a writer of fantasy and science fiction, I can imagine no greater joy than someone reading my work and being inspired to create something of their own – to dream a new dream. As the *Loveletter* says, "This is the love of God."

THE DOMINION OF HUMANITY

It would be tempting to suggest that Christianity look to its own "obscure texts" to find a new way to interpret the Genesis account, but a closer reading of the extant text can be instructive.

Over the course of the first two chapters of Genesis, God speaks, or is recounted to speak, 18 times. Most of these include the "let there be" fiats, or naming of creation (Day, Night etc). But God's words when creating humanity include the Divine purpose: "Let us make humankind in our image, according to our likeness; and let them have dominion over the fish of the sea, and over the birds of the air, and over the cattle, and over all the wild animals of the earth, and over every creeping thing that creeps upon the earth."[25] After creating the first humans, God commands them, "Be fruitful and multiply, and fill the earth and subdue it; and have dominion over the fish of the sea and over the birds of the air and over every living thing that moves upon the earth...See I have given you every plant yielding seed that is upon the face of all the earth and every tree with seed in its fruit; you shall have them for food."[26] It is interesting to note that human subjection of the created order (Heb. *kabash*, Strong's 3533, G/K 3899; tread down, conquer, subjugate) and resulting dominion (Heb. *radah*, Strong's 7287, G/K 8097; tread down, prevail against, reign) is for the purpose of food. In the second creation account, God "took the man and put him in the garden of Eden to till and keep it."[27] The word *keep* (Heb. *shamar*, Strong's 8104, G/K 9068; hedge about, guard, protect, attend to) is the same word used in 3:24 when God placed an angel "and a sword flaming and turning to *guard* the way to the tree of life" (emphasis mine). Human dominion, then, is related not only to human sustenance, but to the protection and stewardship – one dares to say *care* – of the creation.[28]

What is interesting is how that *shamar* is expressed.

A number of the passages where God speaks include "naming" passages, where God gives a name to something created (e.g.1:5 "Day" and "Night"). One of the first tasks for the man is the naming of animals in 2:19-20. Naming is no small business. As many feminist writers have noted, naming defines a thing, indeed, it is a kind of prophecy.[29] This is not always a negative thing. Carol Meyers points out the Hebrew name for the first human (*ha'adam*) is a pun. The word for 'earth' in Hebrew is *'adamah* and it is not difficult to see the similarity to *ha'adam*. For Meyers, *ha'adam* indicates something about the very nature of the first human and, indeed, of all humans – they are taken from the red earth that is able to absorb water, can be cultivated and support life.[30] However, naming can also be used as an act of power. Of Eve's naming by Adam, Trible says, "this language…chillingly echoes the vocabulary of dominion over the animals…there the earth-creature called the name (*sem*) of each animal (2:19). Now, in effect, the man reduces the woman to the status of an animal by calling her a name."[31]

In Genesis 2:19, God brings the animals "to the man to see what he would call them; and whatever the man called every living creature, that was its name." Whereas the power of naming, definition or prophecy of self had, heretofore, been the dominion of God alone, God now gives this dominion to the first human. The enormity of this act cannot be overemphasized. The definition, indeed self-hood, of the created order now lay in the hands of the human: "whatever the man called every living creature, that was its name." Critics may suggest that animals are unaffected by the names we give them (dogs, for instance, are happy to see us whether their name is "Sparky" or "Theopneumatikon"), but that is not the point; part of the creative action of Genesis comes from the naming of the creation and that power (dominion) now rested in the hands of human beings. Naming something is not only an expression of how we view something, but also a prophecy of how we will interact with it – the owner who names their dog "Stupid" or "Dogshit" has and will have little respect for the animal.[32] By naming, humans would now define the creation and, thereby, their interaction with it; humans would become God's coworkers in creation.

But the *shamar* of humanity extends far beyond naming and failure to recognize its extent has led to misunderstanding the Fall. To gain better insight we will need to temporarily leave the creation narrative and look to the New Testament.

THE POEIMA OF GOD

As he was discussing God's sovereign work in saving humanity in Ephesians 2, Paul said, "For we are what he has made us, created in Christ Jesus for good works, which God prepared beforehand to be our way of life."[33] The translator's word choice is interesting here and considering other translations can be instructive. The King James reads, "For we are his workmanship, created in Christ Jesus unto good works, which God hath before ordained that we should walk in them." The NIV, "For we are God's workmanship, created in Christ Jesus to do good works, which God prepared in advance for us to do." Some of the differences are blatant, others subtle.

The Greek word translated "what he made us" and "workmanship" is *poiema* (Strong's 4161, G/K 4473; thing that is made), a word used for mundane objects (chairs) but also for works of art. A number of scholars, artists and musicians have reflected on the meaning of this word when applied to the Christian life. [34] In his essay "Some Perspectives on Art," Francis Schaeffer writes, "No work of art is more important than the Christian's own life, and every Christian is called upon to be an artist in this sense...the Christian's life is to be an art work. The Christian's life is to be a thing of truth and also a thing of beauty in the midst of a lost and despairing world."[35] Human beings, then, are not simply God's "chairs", but God's poems, paintings, sculptures.

The word translated "good works" is *ergon* (Strong's 2041, G/K 2239; deed, action) and is especially interesting in that its plural form, as in 2:10, can denote "history" or "history-as-work."[36] The English word is unfortunate as "work" usually makes us think of the most unpleasant 40 hours of our week, of raking leaves or cleaning up garbage. But "work" can be joyous, especially "good" works.

Finally, the word translated "our way of life", "should walk in them" and "to do" is *peripateo* (Strong's 4043, G/K 4482; walk, be occupied with). It can reference both the more literal "walk," as in ambulation, but also the more figurative "way of life" (both as in occupation or C.S. Lewis' *Tao* in *The Abolition of Man*).[37]

Taken together, we see that we are God's diverse creations, created in Christ to create good and beautiful works that we both walk in and have as our way of living.

I do not think it is going too far to suggest this passage tells us that God created us to create, indeed, to continue the act of creations *and that our creations would be the world in which we lived.* As J.R.R. Tolkien said in his poem *Mythopoeia,*

> *Though all the crannies of the world we filled*
> *With Elves and Goblins, though we dared to build*
> *Gods in their houses out of dark and light*
> *And sowed the seed of dragons, 'twas our right*
> *(used or misused) the right has not decayed.*
> *We make still by the law in which we're made.*[38]

The *shamar* of humanity, then, is not simply an act of administration, but also of creation. The *ha'adam* does not merely name the creatures or, indeed, the creation, but shapes them, develops them, determines their growth. It is as obvious as considering animal husbandry, but also in deforestation. We continue the creative acts of God – the responsibility has been placed in our hands by the Creator Himself – and we live in the world we create. As was said in the movie *Cloud Atlas,* "by each crime and every kindness, we birth our future."

Taken from this perspective, the Fall looks considerably different. Under the meta-narrative of Authority and Obedience, the sin of Adam is an act of defiance against the Creator, an assertion of selfhood apart from God's design. But through this lens, the action of Adam is the willful marring of Creation: Adam is creating a darker, painful world from the "very good" that God made. Indeed, Scripture implies the cursing of the ground is a direct consequence of Adam's action. While God does say that He would place enmity between the serpent and the woman and increase the woman's suffering in childbearing, it nowhere indicates that the cursing of the ground is God's punishment, rather "cursed is the ground *because of you*" (emphasis mine). God, from this perspective, is not punishing Adam, but announcing the consequences of his creation.[39]

In a sense, this is a fairly radical approach, but in some ways almost self-evident. It has profound implications for our reflections on doctrine, especially harmartiology. It also offers a disturbing answer to the problem of evil: there is evil because we created a world that enables it. Perhaps most promising is the new light it casts on the work of Christ, whose redemption extends not only to humanity, but to the transformation of all creation. "For the creation was subjected to futility, not of its own will but by the will of the one who subjected it, in the hope that the creation itself will be set free from its bondage to decay and will obtain the freedom of the glory of the children of God." [40] For those who have long struggled with the doctrine of hell, this perspective suggests that hell may be something we create: around us in the world, but within ourselves as well. Sin and damnation become not matters of punishment for disobedience, but living with the horrors we create. I feel it is important to note here that I am in no way suggesting we jettison the orthodox understandings of these doctrines – I am not creating a new gospel – but am only suggesting a different lens by which to understand our often-mysterious faith. Imagination can open new doors of insight; art may not *be* theology, but it may *reflect* upon theology and give theology new ways of understanding.[41]

But there is something else this perspective tells us. It shows us the magnitude of the human *shamar*, but also reveals the glory and beauty of the human being as God's *poiema*. Most importantly, we discover something about God Himself.

We are the dreams of God that dream new dreams.

"This is the love of God."

Which is not to suggest that the God of the Bible is an everlasting hypnogogic eternally falling in love with Himself or that I AM AND I ARE ALL WE. Rather, that God delights in the Divine creativity, especially as expressed through and by His creations. God created the framework of the creation and then handed it to us to see what we would do with it. And if our artistic choices, let alone our moral ones, have not been the best…well, God is in the work of redemption. "…the pot he was shaping from the clay was marred in his hands; so the potter formed it into another pot, shaping it as seemed best to him."[42]

CONCLUSIONS

There is a special power in beginnings. But there is a special power to the journey as well. If I don't like where my walk is taking me, I can change course.[43] I can also retrace my steps and begin again. Standing back at my front door, I will find the same world waiting for me, the same possibilities. They were, of course, always there even when I didn't see them half-way down the street. But going back to the beginning helped me see them.

Those who play *The Elder Scrolls* games may not take much note of the meta-theme of Stasis and Change – it's one that appears in our world as well, especially in politics. They are not likely to find Lorkhan's call to love in any blatant way – but they are likely to fall in love with the game. Those of us who have spent hours (more than we'd like to admit) wandering the frozen lands of Skyrim, or the ashy wastes of Vvardenfell can attest to the deep longing inside us. We want to go there; we've tasted what it means to "live another life in another world" and want to with a powerful desperation. And this, I suspect, "is the love of God."

Generations of Christians have looked at God as an authority figure to be feared and that fear has distorted our relationship to the Divine. It may be that God will hold us to account for how we have used His creation; it may be that there will be rewards and punishments. It may also be that the world – oceans, frogs, falcons, sharks, sulfur, coal, mountains, volcanoes, the very air – are a gift. They are the palette of God's creativity, given to us to see what we will paint. We have not painted so kindly, it is true. And if we tremble with the words "the fear of the LORD", perhaps we might dare to hope that the beginning of that fear is to love what He created. This, too, is the love of God.

Creation begins and ends with love. And with joy. The brush seems to move of its own accord, the words spill unbidden and un-thought upon the page, the fingers find their way into soft clay all by themselves. And as we stand back, we see that which we ourselves only partially created; creation birthed itself: our dreams dreaming their own dreams. In this moment, we touch upon a joy so deep, so all-encompassing that's its Source can barely be spoken, but it can be felt. His smile lights the stars dotting the firmament, His laughter spills over us like waves upon a beach, His eyes glitter like sparks in fire. We have entered into the joy of our Lord.

What will we do with what has been given us? What world will we create? There are hues uncountable, the canvas waiting and the Master steps back to watch our strokes. They will not be perfect; they will be hesitant, perhaps not a little childish. We may be tempted to throw the palette away, rend the ugly painting. It seems so horrible in our eyes. But the Master will calmly stand, restoring the easel and gently say, "Try again."

Art requires patience. Technique, intuition, grace; these come in time – time and endless practice. The Master may take our hands in His, showing us techniques we never dreamed, but then He will step away and watch as our strokes become more certain, our timbres more subtle. We will learn to be elegant. And when we turn, not a little afraid, to bashfully ask what the Master thinks, He will gaze at all we have labored for, all we have toiled through. Will we see the hint of His smile? Will we feel terror at the hint of His frown? In the end, He will look upon our works and say, "It is beautiful."

BIBLIOGRAPHY - PRINT

Bal, Mieke. *Lethal Love.* Indiana University Press: Bloomington, 1987.

Bulfinch, Thomas. *Bulfinch's Greek and Roman Mythology: The Age of Fable.* Dover Publications: Mineola, 2000.

Ebel, Gunther. "Walk, Run, Way, Conduct." *New International Dictionary of New Testament Theology, The.* Volume 3. Colin Brown, General Editor. Zondervan, Grand Rapids, 1986.

Erickson, Millard. *Christian Theology.* Baker Book House: Grand Rapids, 1983.

Goodrick, Edward W. & John R. Kohlenberger III. *The NIV Exhaustive Concordance.* Zondervan: Grand Rapids, 1990.

Guthrie, Shirley C. Jr. *Christian Doctrine.* Westminster John Knox Press: Louisville, 1994.

Gyatso, Tenzin. *The World of Tibetan Buddhism.* Translated by Geshe Thupten Jinpa. Wisdom Publications: Boston, 1995.

Hahn, Hans-Christop et al. "Work, Do, Accomplish." *New International Dictionary of New Testament Theology, The.* Volume 3. Colin Brown, General Editor. Zondervan, Grand Rapids, 1986.

Meyers, Carol. Discovering Eve. Oxford University Press: New York. 1988.

New Oxford Annotated Bible. Edited by Michael D. Coogan. Oxford University Press: Oxford. 2007.

Pagels, Elaine. *The Gnostic Gospels.* Vintage Books: New York, 1979.

Schaeffer, Francis A. "Some Perspectives on Art." *Art and the Bible.* IVP Books: Downers Grove, 1973.

Strong, James. *Strong's Exhaustive Concordance of the Bible.* World Bible Publishers, Inc, 1986.

Tolkien, J.R.R. "On Faerie Stories." *The Tolkien Reader.* Ballantine Books: New York, 1966.

Trible, Phyllis. *God and the Rhetoric of Sexuality*. Fortress Press: Philadelphia, 1978.

BIBLIOGRAPHY – INTERNET

Deluzain, H. Edward. "Names and Personality." Retrieved at *http://www.behindthename.com/articles/2.php* on 7 December 2011.

Loveletter From the Fifth Era, The True Purpose of Tamriel. *http://www.imperial- library.info/content/loveletter-fifth-era-true-purpose-tamriel*. Imperial Library site. Retrieved 4-15-2013

MacDonald, George. A Dish of Orts. *http://www2.hn.psu.edu/faculty/jmanis/gmacdonald/a- dish-of-orts6x9.pdf*. Retrieved 7-29-3013.

Monomyth, The. h*ttp://www.imperial-library.info/content/monomyth* Imperial Library site. Retrieved 4-15-2013

Metaphysics of Morrowind, The. *http://fallingawkwardly.wordpress.com/2010/08/29/the- metaphysics-of-morrowind-part-1/ Falling Awkwardly blog*. Retrieved 4-23-2013.

Sithis. http://www.uesp.net/wiki/Lore:Sithis_(book) Unofficial Elder Scrolls Page site. Retrieved 4-15-2013.

Thirty-Six Lessons of Vivec, The. *http://www.imperial-library.info/node/1259/* Imperial Library site. Retrieved 4-15-2013

Vehk's Teachings. *http://www.imperial-library.info/content/vehks-teaching* Imperial Library site. Retrieved 4-13-2013.

Endnotes

[1] Of course not all religious traditions focus on a revelation of deity through Creation, but all draw life-patterns from their earliest (often creation) stories. The Greek and Roman mythoi begin with the ordering of chaos, a not inapt metaphor (and thereby justification) for empires forging civilization from unenlightened "barbarism" (Bulfinch 10). In the Norse myth, life is born from (and supported by) the omnipresent ice, not unexpected from a people living in cold northern climes. That the world-tree Ygdrasill, which supports the universe, sprung from the first creature's body (Ymir) suggests a theme of life, death, and re-birth which may have had

particular significance to a culture where arctic winters and springs were a yearly reminder of this cycle (Bulfinch 264-5). In all mythoi, however, beginnings reveal the course of future narratives, and often the purpose(s) of both gods and mortals.

[2] *http://www.imperial-library.info/content/monomyth*

[3] But not all; some of the spirits refused Lorkhan's call and became the Daedra (Elvish, "not our ancestors") .

[4] This is especially true of the Valentinian gnostics who saw the flesh as something to be released from (*http://www.gnosis.org/library/valentinus/Valentinian_Creation.htm*). As will be seen in the discussion on the Psijic Endeavor below, certain sects of Altmer saw the finding of the "ur-you" as a form of transcendence, paralleling with the author of the Gospel of Phillip for whom seeing God was to become God (Pagels 134). There are, of course, numerous "Gnosticisms" and not all would fit into this Altmeri view, but similarities persist.

[5] Or the Aedra (Elvish, "our ancestors"); the et'Ada are worshipped as gods by the people of Tamriel.

[6] Erickson page 373; of particular note is the way Erickson sees creation obeying God by rebuking the disobedient Jonah.

[7] The note for 1:3 in the New Oxford Annotated Bible is instructive: "Like a divine king God pronounces his will and it is accomplished."

[8] Genesis 2:17.

[9] Genesis 6:5, 6.

[10] Ecclesiastes 12:13, 14.

[11] See especially Rita Nakashima Brock and Rebecca Ann Parker's *Proverbs of Ashes* for a Feminist perspective.

[12] And indeed it is a problem that has haunted Christianity throughout its history. Numerous attempts have been made to examine Christ's redemptive work from different angles; Gustaf Aulen's *Christus Victor* gives an excellent history. I am not here dismissing these views – far from it – but am suggesting that on some level all struggle against the Biblical narrative's model of substitutionary atonement (spiritual cleansing via sacrifice; Christ as "the lamb of God who takes away the sin of the world"). In this way I see the model I am presenting as one in a long series of attempts to view Christ's work from multiple angles. For more contemporary readings consider Monica A. Coleman's *Making a Way Out of No Way*, Matthew Fox's *Creation Spirituality*, and Gustavo Guitierrez's *A Theology of Liberation*. For a popular fictional treatment William Paul Young's The Shack is worth noting.

[13] The elvish name for Akatosh.

[14] Sithis is the elvish name for Padomay.

[15] It is difficult not to think of the Un-man's speeches to the Green Lady in Lewis' *Perelandra*, even if Lorkhan's motives are kinder than the possessed scientist's.

[16] Of course those passionate about TES lore – meeting on the online Lore Forums – debate among themselves to what extent the Obscure Texts should be accepted as "canon" to the game, much as early Christians argued about what books belonged in the Scriptural canon. Consensus of opinion has been hard to come by but, in a fascinating parallel to Christian history, many of the "loremasters" (long-time fans who are deeply passionate about the games' lore) have tended to accept Obscure Texts based on their authorship – works written by game developers, or those with extensive knowledge of lore, are generally accepted by the Lore community as "canon". It remains to be seen if future games will contradict, or confirm, the Obscure Texts.

[17] See especially the Metaphysics of Morrowind where the author suggests Vivec knows he is in a "simulacrum of reality" or video game, and comments about it in his writings and in-game conversations with the player. *http://fallingawkwardly.wordpress.com/2010/08/29/the-metaphysics-of-morrowind-part-1/*

[18] That is, Padomay.

[19] The Aurbis is the whole of creation, comprised (ultimately) of Aetherius, Oblivion, and Nirn.

[20] For more on the Wheel see Sermon 21 of Vivec's *Thrity-Six Lessons: http://www.imperial-library. info/node/1259/*

[21] Understanding what Lorkhan saw and why it was so important to him is difficult. Lorkhan was, according to Vivec, dissatisfied with the cyclical and impermanent nature of the universe – the same ideas swirling around again and again. It might be said that Lorkhan found each moment of creation inexpressibly beautiful but that beauty faded as each creation fell into predictable patterns; perhaps the worst of these was the pattern of birth, death, and re-birth. Coming to the edge of creation (beginning and ending) Lorkhan beheld the whole and beheld the Wheel. There is considerable disagreement about what this means. For some Lorkhan saw himself as yet another repeating pattern devoid of meaning or originality, for some he beheld the truth that he was nothing more (or less) than a dream in the mind of a sleeping Godhead, and for others that Lorkhan saw he was an idea in a video game. It is not going too far, I think, to compare Lorkhan's vision of the Wheel with Neo's realization that he had been living in a computer simulation in *The Matrix.* "The relentless alien terror that is God", then, is the realization that one's personhood is an illusion: Lorkhan was not a person but zero's and one's of computer code. The Tower is this realization, and as Vivec explains, achieving the Tower's secret is being able to see yourself in this way and still be able to say "I am." In an interesting exchange in the first *Matrix* Neo struggles with the life he lived in the simulation and what it means. Trinity observes, "the Matrix cannot tell you who you are." A Lorkhanic response from Neo would have been, "The Matrix showed me that I am Neo, and Neo I am still."

[22] See especially the excellent series of articles "The Metaphysics of Morrowind", above. This is not an unusual thing in gaming: the "Implementors" of the Infocom games, have been seen by some as in-game representations of the game's developers.

[23] From *The Loveletter from the Fifth Era, the True Purpose of Tamriel, http://www.imperial-library. info/content/loveletter-fifth-era-true-purpose-tamriel*

[24] "A *bodhisattva* is a person who cultivates the aspiration to achieve complete enlightenment for the benefit of all living beings and who has also pledged to engage in the deeds that are the most beneficial in fulfilling this aim of working for others." (Gyatso 89). The Dalai Lama, of course, is writing from within a Tibetan Buddhist framework; Theravada Buddhism sees the work of a bodhisattva differently.

[25] Genesis 1:26

[26] Genesis 1:28, 29

[27] Genesis 2:15

[28] For a notable consideration of this see Shirley C. Guthrie, Jr's *Christian Doctrine*, pages 148-9.

[29] Bal 73. See also H. Edward Deluzain's article "Names and Personality": "The most important aspect of personality affected by names is self-concept. Self-concept develops as children develop, and it is 'learned' from the verbal and non-verbal messages significant people in children's lives send them. Parents are the most important message-senders, but, as children mature and become more and more independent, the messages of teachers, classmates, and other people all contribute to their developing concepts of self. In a sense, self-concept works as a kind of script for the way people act. If a boy has an image of himself as bad or as not capable of doing well in school, his behavior will probably reflect that image. He will tend to behave the way he thinks a 'bad boy' is supposed to behave, or he will fail to learn as he should even though he might be quite intelligent" (Behind the Name website)

[30] Meyers 81-82. Puns are common in Hebrew. In this case the name of the first human could also be a pun on a pun on *dam* "blood" and *edom* "red".

[31] Trible 135

[32] Note that several Biblical characters have their names changed after significant encounters with God (Jacob becomes Israel in Genesis 32:27-28; and Saul of Tarsus becomes Paul in Acts 13:9).

[33] Ephesians 2:10

[34] See especially Michael Card's reflection in his album *Poiema*, but also (more subtly) in Francis Schaeffer's work *Art and the Bible*.

[35] Schaeffer 94

[36] Hahn et al. 1147

[37] Ebel 943

[38] Tolkien 74

[39] It is supremely significant that Adam's first act following God's pronouncement is to name his wife Eve using the same language as naming the animals. For more on this see Trible, as noted above.

[40] Romans 8:20, 21

[41] "The imagination of man is made in the image of the imagination of God. Everything of man must have been of God first; and it will help much towards our understanding of the imagination and its functions in man if we first succeed in regarding aright the imagination of God, in which the imagination of man lives and moves and has its being." (MacDonald 7)

[42] Jeremiah 18:4

[43] One cannot resist thinking of the Greek word *metanoia* here.

Procedural Theology in The Elder Scrolls Series[1]

By Mark Hayse, Ph.D.

Where is that magic sword? How can I get my hands on more gold? What does it take to defeat that dragon? Every role-playing gamer asks these questions because they constitute the core gameplay of the role-playing game: powering up, leveling up and beating up. These are the things that players must do in order to survive and thrive as heroes in the making. Like all computer role-playing games, *The Elder Scrolls* (ES) series closely adheres to this structure. The ES player climbs a ladder of might and magic, each new gain marking another rung. In order to conquer a game in the ES series, the player's statistical profile must incrementally grow and steadily develop. Gold, experience, skill and reputation points unlock each step that the player takes. As the player explores Tamriel--the fictional land of the ES series- gameplay inevitably produces statistical gains. Even though players celebrate the ES series for its sense of open-ended possibility, its gameplay still launches players on quests to accrue points. The ES series encourages players to roam freely and explore deeply in Tamriel, yet it stubbornly confronts players with foes to defeat. Can players enjoy the ES series without ever "winning" a game by beating the final boss? Yes. Can players escape statistical gains along the way? Not for long.

At first glance, this insight may seem relatively unimportant in light of the narrative elements of the ES series--its themes, dialogues and unfolding mysteries. Indeed, many of the essays in this present volume focus upon the rich theological significance of mythology and symbolism throughout the ES series. It abounds in narrative complexity and it begs for careful interpretive analysis. However, narrative approaches to video game analysis cannot account for all layers of meaning within the medium. Narrative analyses are helpful, even crucial. Nevertheless, procedural approaches to video game analysis also bear much fruit. Video game rules and structures elicit certain kinds of behavior from players while prohibiting other kinds of behavior. This essay uses the word "procedure" to describe the kinds of behaviors elicited by video game rules and structures. Video game procedures may not draw as much attention as the narrative elements of gameplay, even though they exert a steady influence upon gameplay, moment by moment. The procedural aspect of gameplay tends to function at a more implicit level than narrative aspects, thus rendering them harder to recognize and harder to analyze.

This essay identifies and analyzes the core procedures that constitute gameplay throughout the ES series, contemplating their meaning. The first section of the essay clarifies the terms of discussion, such as "implicit curriculum" and "procedure." Next, the essay recounts the procedural evolution of the ES series. Following that, the essay presents a "procedural archeology" of the precedents that undergird the ES series, such as the historical wargame, the tabletop role-playing game, the military development of computer technology and the video game system. The essay then turns toward an analysis of "procedural theology"--an implicit curriculum arguably embedded within the ES series' procedural structure.

IMPLICIT CURRICULUM AND VIDEO GAME PROCEDURES

Video games are learning environments (Gee 2007; Squire 2011) in which players master a unique kind of curriculum, not through tiresome lectures but through active experience. However, much curriculum is implicit, subtle or hidden, whether in the learning environment of the classroom or video game. Philip Jackson (1968) describes the implicit curriculum as a set of values, subtly embedded within the "rules, regulations, and routines" of the learning environment. Jackson goes on to say that students (or by extension, players) indirectly learn the implicit curriculum through the reinforcement of "crowds, praise, and power" (p. 33-36). To paraphrase Jackson, students learn that which their environment values and celebrates. Learning environments teach not only *what* to learn (the explicit curriculum), but *how* to learn (the implicit curriculum). They teach not only *what* to think, but *how* to think. For example, timetables, schedules, desk arrangements and seating charts all imply a way of learning, exerting a quiet influence upon student behavior (see for example, Cuban 1995; Goodlad 2004). More colorfully, Roland Meighan (1981) describes the implicit curriculum as a "haunted curriculum" in which the "ghosts" of classroom architects and curriculum writers still exert a powerful influence upon unquestioning students in learning environments. Maxine Greene (1983) further argues that the implicit curriculum compels students into "an unthinking, nonreflective acceptance of what is presented as a social destiny" (p. 4). In summary, the physical and social structures of each learning environment shape students in their own image, capturing their imaginations along the way. Students may interrogate the explicit curriculum, but most of the time they "play along" with the implicit curriculum.

During gameplay, video game procedures operate as a kind of implicit curriculum. They tell players how to play and how not to play. Push the joystick to move forward. Press the button to pick up the sword and swing it. Click the icon to consult the character profile. Rules and structures such as these are, quite literally, "standard operating procedure" for video games, such as the ES series. Of course, players tend to take procedures like these for granted. These procedures comprise the elemental foundation of play that makes possible life in a virtual world and yet, they are relatively uninteresting. Players take procedures for granted as the invisible infrastructure of virtual reality. Along these lines, Ian Bogost (2006) argues that whole game engines--the interconnected systems of video game procedures--inevitably "construe entire gameplay behavior" (p. 57). For example, Bogost notes that most game engines reflect a design that supports "visual and physical experience rather than emotional and interpersonal experience" (p. 64). In other words, most game engines do better at establishing procedures for movement and collision than for love and intimacy.

Bogost and others (see also Frasca 2004; Squire 2011) argue that video game procedures subtly present ideological points of view. Put another way, they present models of the world, as well as rules for engagement with the world. Most video games do not explicitly present a model of so-called "real life." Nevertheless, Bogost argues that video games cannot help but depict "some small subset of the natural world, in a necessarily biased manner" (p. 97). As cultural artifacts, video games reflect the viewpoints and values of their makers. Furthermore, video game sequels reflect a digital inheritance from the procedural engines upon which they stand (2007, p. 112). Returning to the discussion above, video game procedures are "haunted" by the design of those who have gone before. For better or worse, they bear the marks of previous programmers. They reflect the choices of earlier decision makers. When the designers of "Version 1.0" decide that Pac-Man (Namco 1980) must eat the dot, that Mario must collect coins (Nintendo 1985) or that the player of *DOOM* (id Software 1993) must shoot anything that moves, then the designers of Versions 2.0, 3.0 and so on inherit and amplify those design decisions. Players of these games do not choose whether to eat dots, jump on heads or kill enemies. Instead, they take these procedures for granted. These procedures are the rules of engagement. Thus, video game procedures enjoy a highly privileged place of influence in gameplay. Bogost argues that "the highly polished visual and sound design" of video games draw players' attention like moths to light, "thus rendering [procedures] implicit and in need of critique" (p. 113). This is why Bogost concludes that "the most important moment in the study of a videogame" is the procedural moment (2006, p. 99).

PROCEDURAL EVOLUTION
WITHIN THE ELDER SCROLLS SERIES

The procedures of the ES series grow in complexity across two decades of evolution, from their humble beginnings in *The Elder Scrolls: Arena* to the more sophisticated *The Elder Scrolls: Skyrim*. Yet, these games are deeply rooted within a common procedural logic, haunted by a common structure despite innovations across time. Below, each of the five main games in the ES receives a critical assessment. Fans of the series may struggle to read an extended critique of something that they hold dear. After all, the ES series enjoys many well-deserved awards for its expansive worlds, provocative stories, ethical dilemmas and deep mythology. Nevertheless, this essay casts a narrower focus upon the implicit procedural structures of the five main games in the ES series.

In *The Elder Scrolls: Arena* (1994), the player begins by selecting one of 18 character classes and one of eight races. Each class and race generates a different statistical profile in terms of available skills, weapons, armor, shields and starting health points. Following this, the player distributes points among eight governing attributes: Strength, Intelligence, Willpower, Agility, Speed, Endurance, Personality and Luck. When viewing the character profile screen, the player must not only monitor all of these statistical values, but also bonuses to damage, magic defense, general defense, general attack, charisma and healing, along with fatigue points, gold pieces, experience points, class level and the maximum weight that he is able to carry. As the player begins to explore the lay of the land and fights many foes, this statistical profile grows stronger over time. Every weapon, every spell, every piece of armor and every magical item either raises or lowers some aspect of this profile. Thus, strategic statistical management is central to game play.

The player also uses a computer mouse in order to navigate game space. The mouse enables movement and it establishes interaction with persons and objects. Throughout gameplay, the player uses the mouse to identify, equip, unequip, buy, sell, pick up, drop and swap literally thousands of items. Mouse in hand, the player must repeatedly click eight icons at the bottom of the screen. These icons define the procedural heart and soul of gameplay: attacking enemies, casting spells, stealing items, using items, consulting a travel journal, consulting a map, consulting the statistical profile and resting in order to replenish statistical loss.

According to the Player Guide, magic spells stand at "the crux of the world of *Arena*." The box art for *Arena* promises that the game's unique Spellmaker system allows the player to "create thousands of spells from over 80 combinable effects." A well-equipped spell book will effectively boost the player's statistical advantage in combat, albeit temporarily. Spell book in hand, the player increases damage dealt to others, reduces damage to self, destroys or bypasses obstacles such as walls, floors, and locks, and absorbs the statistical strengths of enemies. In short, the magic system of *Arena* enables statistical manipulation. Every friend, foe and object either enriches or depletes the player's statistical strength. Magic maximizes statistical benefits while minimizing statistical costs.

The *Arena* Player's Guide and box art colorfully identify the overarching goals of gameplay: exploring and fighting. For example, the Player's Guide reads:

> "We have given the world many areas of exploration, over four hundred places where death can be dealt in new and exciting ways. It is a place where those of you who love combat and spell casting can earn fame and fortune by proving your prowess in battle."

Likewise, *Arena's* box art promises the twin thrills of discovery and violence:

> "Over 8 million square kilometers" of undiscovered country awaits, from "the fertile fields of Summerset Isle" to "the frozen mists of Skyrim."

> "Confront fearsome adversaries as you make your way to the Staff of Chaos...Battle Monsters (sic) of the netherworld, using any of 2500 magical items...."

In the final analysis, the gameplay procedures of *Arena* hinge upon discovery, combat and statistical management. On the surface, *Arena* provides the player with a measure of procedural "freedom"--freedom to select male or female, freedom to select thief or warrior or mage, freedom to shop for more equipment than one person could use in a lifetime, freedom to explore a vast countryside at will and freedom to fight or flee. Players enthusiastically celebrate this measure of freedom. However, Howegameplay in *Arena* also suffers from procedural constriction. No matter which gender or race the player may choose, the ongoing obligation of statistical management awaits. The player may feel free to explore the whole wide world, but many of the game's mysteries remain hidden away until the achievement of sufficient statistical gains through the spoils of war. Put simply, the *Arena* player lives to fight and fights to live, no matter which direction he goes.

More briefly considered, *The Elder Scrolls: Daggerfall* (1996) extends the procedural gameplay of *Arena*. The box art promises, "The largest world ever created by a computer role-playing game" featuring "thousands of cities, villages, dungeons, graveyards, ruins, castles, shrines and farms". In addition, the player may interact with numerous characters through dialogue and action. *Daggerfall* also adds greater complexity to the enchantment of equipment and to the political milieu of guilds and religions. Like *Arena*, however, *Daggerfall* suffers from procedural constriction. Gameplay forces the player to grind through exhausting waves of enemies in order to earn more and more points, thereby unlocking the whole game. The basic gameplay of strategic statistical management remains the same. The greater geographical and statistical complexity of *Daggerfall* renders it much richer than *Arena*, but its procedural structure remains the same: powering up, leveling up and beating up.

In the same way, *The Elder Scrolls III: Morrowind* (2002) and *The Elder Scrolls IV: Oblivion* (2006) extend the procedural gameplay of their predecessors. Once again, the box art promises:

> "The enormous game world is open and free for you to discover. Go anywhere you want and do anything you want."

"The entire world of Oblivion is open for you to explore at your own pace."

Nevertheless, the basic gameplay of grinding through level upon level of strategic statistical management remains essentially unchanged, even though both games introduce interesting innovations. For example, *Morrowind* and *Oblivion* rely upon a two-stage skill system of primary statistics and secondary abilities. They introduce a "birthsign" that adds special statistical abilities to the player's character. They incorporate a process of gradual deterioration to weapons and armor, while mana points (for magic) gradually regenerate over time. In the final analysis, these innovations do not change the ES series reliance upon statistical management. Instead, they merely amplify its complexity. As mentioned above, it is impossible to uncover the secrets of Tamriel apart from steady statistical growth. Exploration, combat and skill development fuel statistical growth, while statistical growth enables greater progress in exploration and combat. Imps, wolves and skeletons, for example, present a decreasing challenge to the player as the game progresses. In contrast, Daedra pose a much greater challenge to the player when they appear later in the game. In all of these cases, the ES series drives its player into violent conflict.

The Elder Scrolls V: Skyrim (2011) attempts radical surgery on the procedural structure of the ES series. In one sense, *Skyrim* succeeds. It adds both complexity and simplicity to the statistical management system of the ES series. For example, *Skyrim* repeals the class system, but introduces a system of perks that unlock special abilities. The combat system simplifies the taxonomy of weapons, but adds special "finishing moves" to combat. The spell system no longer allows players to design their own customized spells. Armor and weapons no longer dull over time, although a grindstone or workbench can enhance their strength.

Skyrim eliminates birthsigns, but introduces Guardian Stones that serve a comparable function. *Skyrim* also collapses the eight attributes of *Arena* into a simpler system of three: Health, Magicka and Stamina. Perhaps most significantly, *Skyrim* introduces an innovative story system that generates tailor made side quests into gameplay. However, this system still serves the procedural structure of its predecessors. Each quest enhances the player's statistical profile in one way or another. The box art for *Skyrim* aptly summarizes the procedural system that constitutes gameplay: "Fight dragons and power up!"

Although *The Elder Scrolls* series receives much well-deserved praise for its cutting-edge accomplishments and sophisticated innovations, each of the five main games in the series tightly adheres to a similar procedural structure. The celebrated "freedom" of the ES series suffers from inescapable constriction. The ES series strictly obeys its own procedural law, whether by birthsigns or Guardian Stones, eight attributes or three, classes or perks, linear stories or side-quests. Through any means necessary, players steadily climb the statistical ladder of might and magic: powering up, leveling up and beating up anything that stands in their way.

Toward a Procedural Archeology of The Elder Scrolls Series

Research gives considerable attention to the ancestral militaristic curriculum that implicitly "haunts" video game procedures, up to and including the ES series. The ES series rests upon a long-standing tradition that begins with ancient wargames of the East. In turn, these birth the modern wargames of the West that, in turn, spawn the modern role-playing game (RPG). In the mid-Twentieth Century, the US military designs the computer to perform statistical calculations for wargames, a machine that profoundly informs the design of the video game system and the computer role-playing game (CRPG). This discussion begs for a lengthier treatment than allowed in this essay. However, those who wish to read further may consult Toles' (1985) early discussion of video games, military training and American military ideology, Lenoir's (2000) critique of the military-entertainment complex, Halter's (2006) assessment of war and video games, Barton's (2008) history of the CRPG; Deterding's (2010) historical survey of wargaming board games as the antecedent to wargaming computer games, Donovan's (2010) general history of video games, and especially Crogan's (2011) incisive analysis of the reciprocal relationship between computer games, war, simulation and technoculture. Drawing upon these sources, the paragraphs below briefly outline the contours of an "archeological dig" into the procedural precedents of the ES series, with a focus upon wargaming and military logic.

Halter traces the history of wargaming across cultures and time to the present day. From ancient China's *Go* to ancient India's *chaturanga* to medieval Europe's chess, all cultures and kings seem to have played at war. European chess led to a more complex simulation of war, utilizing miniature terrain, unit measurements and combat maneuvers. In the 19th century, Prussian military officers developed the modern *kriegspiel* or "wargame" which the US military adapted soon after. Soon, even children learned to play these miniature wargames with the use of household toys and introductory rulebooks, such as H. G. Wells' *Floor Games* ([1911] 2006) and *Little Wars* ([1913] 2004). Barton further notes that the Twentieth Century witnessed the introduction of the first mass-market wargame, *Tactics*, along with the founding of Avalon Hill--a primary publisher of wargames and strategy games to the present day.

Barton tells the story of how Gary Gygax and his associates developed a medieval miniatures wargame named *Chainmail*, soon followed by the RPG *Dungeons & Dragons*. In *Dungeons & Dragons*, Gygax and others introduced "several key innovations to the established wargaming model," including single characters, character classes, experience points, leveling up, hit points and a Dungeon Master to referee the burden of statistical calculation throughout gameplay (p. 19-21). Barton contends that these innovations created a tension that persists to this day in the RPG. On one hand, wargaming emphasizes strategy and tactics. On the other hand, role-playing emphasizes story, character and dialogue. As a mix of both wargaming and role-playing, the RPG holds them together as one. Nevertheless, Barton contends that "all fantasy role-playing games require a statistics-based rule system to provide structure for the playacting and make believe; without them, the game would seem hopelessly arbitrary and probably not much fun to play" (p. 22). Barton's work situates the history of the CRPG within the history of the RPG and the wargame. In addition, Deterding tells the same story, but with a different purpose, nicely complementing Barton.

Donovan and Halter argue that American military wargaming spawned the invention of the computer and the video game. Donovan explains that the onset of the Cold War saw the introduction of ENIAC (Electronic Numerical Integrator and Computer), created in order to calculate artillery-firing tables for the US Army. Within months, the Dumont Television Network developed a prototype for video play on home television sets. Their Cathode-Ray Tube Amusement Device allowed players to attach physical targets to the television screen in order to fire video missiles at them. The cathode-ray tube drew the lines of missile trajectory and created simulated explosions on the screen. Within ten to fifteen years, scientists at the Brookhaven National Laboratory and Massachusetts Institute of Technology created mainframe video games upon the same procedural foundations: statistical calculation, tactical movement, missile trajectories and missile collisions. In similar fashion, Ralph Baer's ("The Father of

Video Games") video game prototype included a chase game and a plastic rifle shooting game. Halter colorfully observes that many contemporary video game players naively assess their computer systems with a "decidedly libertarian streak," often failing to acknowledge that video games tend to reflect an implicit, military logic (p. 79).

Likewise, Crogan observes that video game scholarship often overlooks the military logic that informs computer procedures. In his discussion, he contends that the "logistical trajectories" of the computer have "overdetermined" the imaginations of those who design its applications (p. xxv). Crogan claims, "Conflict-based games are arguably the major proportion of commercial computer games," even in game genres that do not claim to be conflict-based (p. xxvi). For example, action games that do not center upon conflict still rely upon a procedural engine that "is nonetheless some variation of tracking, targeting and shooting/acquiring interactions, usually while navigating through a challenging environment" (p. xxvi-xxvii). The first generation of Atari VCS game cartridges (1977) well illustrates the point. Seven of the nine implicitly reflect a procedural structure of military operations--tracking, targeting, shooting and navigating-- whether explicitly violent or not: *Air-Sea Battle, Combat, Indy 500, Star Ship, Street Racer, Surround* and *Video Olympics*. Only *Basic Math* and *Blackjack* divert from this kind of game play, as do some other computer game developments of that era. For example, the more literary text adventure emphasizes puzzle solving and the exploration of virtual space. Nevertheless, Chris Crawford, an Atari designer and forefather of contemporary video game design, rightly observes, "Combat games have always been at the heart of computer gaming" (cited in Halter, p. 87).

The US military continues to sponsor hardware and software developments that inspire video game design while leveraging new developments in video game technologies for training purposes. In her 1985 study, Toles notes that the skills of video game play are highly transferable to a military context. In each case, participants must track, target and shoot the enemy while navigating hostile terrain. Toles also observes that video game interfaces depersonalize aggression toward the enemy through technological means, a useful skill for live combat. Just as Toles explains how US Army officials use video games for military skill development, Lenoir explains (in greater depth) how the US Marines deploy video games such as the first-person shooter *DOOM*, for combat training. Crogan suggests that this relationship between computer games, war and the military is "reciprocal" and "rebounding"--a feedback loop that enhances all involved. Computer games reflect military values and incorporate military practices, even as the military learns from and incorporates computer game practices into its culture of training. To Crogan, computer games reorient users' minds "around the themes of information processing and management...the control of complex situations, the anticipations of contingencies, and the development of reliable problem-solving techniques and technics." (p. 89-90). These tactical, strategic and statistical qualities are not exclusive to the military. Nevertheless, they reflect a military logic of wargaming, amplified in video game procedures.

Lawrence Lessig (2006) writes, "The software and hardware that make cyberspace what it is constitute a set of constraints on how you behave...They constrain some behavior by making other behavior possible or impossible. The code embeds certain values or makes certain values impossible" (p. 124-125). Procedurally, the ES series has not risen above the military logic of the wargame, a logic reflective of early computer design. Conflict rules gameplay. Evasion may briefly prove useful, but direct engagement with the enemy is inevitable. Constantly scanning the environment, the player must identify and eliminate a seemingly infinite parade of enemies. Victory follows the careful statistical analysis of opponents and the strategic management of resources. Rising through the ranks, the player gradually gathers stockpiles of technology that grant an edge in combat. The sheer number of available weapons, armor, magic items, spells and artifacts implies the necessity of violent engagement. Even the tailor made quests of *Skyrim* often lead the player into conflict or violent engagement, whether incidentally or intentionally. The procedural structure of the ES series immerses players within statistical gameplay in the service of violence. Of course, computers can do more than simulate war. Likewise, the ES series is certainly much more than a military simulation. Nevertheless, an implicit curriculum thoroughly "haunts" each game in the series, subtly and profoundly shaping gameplay: powering up, leveling up and beating up.

PROCEDURAL THEOLOGY AND REDEMPTIVE VIOLENCE IN THE ES SERIES

Walter Wink (1992) argues that violence "undergirds American popular culture," the "ethos," "spirituality," "myth" and "religion" that animates entertainment (p. 13). More particularly, Wink contends that the "myth of redemptive violence" rationalizes the nationalistic fervor of every empire that seeks to justify its own violent actions in the name of a greater good. Wink traces the origins of this myth to ancient Babylon. In that religious system, the law god Marduk slays the chaos goddess Tiamat in order to stabilize the gods' heavenly reign. When Marduk dismembers Tiamat's body after her defeat, he unwisely uses her flesh and blood to sow the seeds of Creation. Thus, Marduk tragically fails because the chaos eternally lurks just beneath the surface of an orderly world, springing from Tiamat's very blood. This theological framework animates the military violence of ancient Babylon. Those who oppose the rule of imperial law are the enemy. Those who serve imperial law are heroes. Violence becomes a virtue when done in the king's name. Wink writes, "Salvation *is* politics: identifying with the god of order against the god of chaos, and offering oneself up for the holy war required to impose order and rule..." (p. 16). The powers and principalities sanctify violence as the path to peace, securing in place an ideologically-motivated "Domination System" of imperial privilege and oppression (p. 107).

In contrast, Wink contrasts the Domination System with God's Reign--a "domination-free order characterized by partnership, interdependence, equality of opportunity, and mutual respect..." (p. 107). Within the context of Christian tradition, Jesus announces the end of the Domination System through nonviolent means. From Wink's perspective, Jesus's sacrificial death does not signify God's *final* act of violence, but God's *end* to violence (p. 153-154). Nonviolence lies at the heart of God's Reign revealed in Jesus, a "third way" beyond fight or flight. According to Wink, God's Reign comes through practices such as (p. 186-187):

- Finding creative alternatives to violence
- Asserting the dignity and worth of persons
- Refusing to humiliate others
- Shaming oppressors into repentance
- Suffering willingly instead of wreaking vengeance
- Depriving oppressors of settings in which violence is effective
- Accepting the consequences for breaking unjust laws
- Renouncing fear of the powers and principalities
- Seeking the transformation of the oppressor (p. 186-187)

Wink insists that these practices cast light on a path that resists so-called "holy war" on one hand and naïve inactivity on the other (p. 319-324).

In its most elemental procedural structure, the ES series incorporates a Domination System of redemptive violence in which might makes right. Whether the player aligns with a faction or chooses a path of political free agency, violence follows. In Tamriel, no player gets very far without violence. Justifiably, combat bestows the boon of blood--the experience points, gold pieces and skill points that statistically unlock and enable the pleasure of exploration. The rule set throughout the ES series stands upon a wargaming tradition and a role-playing game tradition that mediate combat by design. From the outset, the player embarks upon a grand adventure of gradual dominance. Various quests grant a dazzling array of rewards that, at first glance, appear quite diverse. Upon closer examination, however, these rewards serve one fundamental purpose: to enhance a statistical profile that will secure victory.

In the Sermon on the Mount, Jesus says, "For wide is the gate and broad is the road that leads to destruction, and many enter it. But small is the gate and narrow the road that leads to life, and only a few enter it" (Matthew 7:13b-14). Throughout gameplay in the ES series, the gate of violent domination is wide indeed. Put another way, the swift current of the Domination System tends to carry the player downstream. This type of gameplay is hard to resist, at least for long. Over time, the player gradually succumbs to that which Wink calls "violent mimesis" (i.e. becoming that which is hated)--a monster slayer whose deadly skills meet or surpass those of the enemy (p. 195-205). Within Christian tradition, the hope of salvation comes, not through violence and domination, but through reconciliation and humility. However, video games such as the ES series tend to celebrate superheroic Caesars rather than cross-shaped Christs (Lawrence and Jewett 2002). This mode of gameplay is nearly impossible to resist.

The apostle Paul writes that Jesus won salvation for all through the weakness and foolishness of the Cross, nullifying "the things that are" through "the things that are not" (1 Corinthians 1:18-31). In short, Jesus' path to glory is cruciform, not coercive (Philippians 2:5-11). However, the cruciform path (Gorman 2001) cannot get a player very far in Tamriel. Throughout all Creation, Jesus' death secures a cosmic victory: the end of our violence and the reconciliation of all things (Romans 12:17-21; Colossians 1:15-20). In Tamriel, however, the player's death means nothing more than a momentary setback to violence, followed by a slap on the back to get up and try again. Without exception, the crucifixion, resurrection and ascension of Jesus ends up parodied in the CRPGs, like the ES series as players inevitably die at the enemy's hands, reload the game and level up to crush their enemies. In the final analysis, the ES series builds its gameplay upon the foundation of an implicit and inescapable procedural theology that is simple in construction, yet far-reaching in its scope: fight fire with fire by powering up, leveling up and beating up.

CONCLUDING REMARKS

This essay strikes a single chord about implicit curriculum, video game procedures and redemptive violence--but that chord constitutes neither an entire melody nor an entire song. To the contrary, much remains unsung about curriculum, video games and theology, certainly more than these paragraphs contain. Curriculum theorists, video game critics and theologians share at least one commonality: their disciplinary discourses inevitably turn into "complicated conversations" (Pinar 2011) about plurality and interdisciplinarity. For example, curriculum theorists wrestle with numerous questions beyond the implicit curriculum, such as questions of politics, race, gender, philosophy, theology, self, perception, science, technology and aesthetics (Pinar, Reynolds, Slattery, and Taubman 2006; Slattery 2013). Likewise, video game critics and theologians wrestle with such questions. No single frame of reference may adequately account for the complexity of meanings. In that spirit, the three comments below (incomplete as they are) seek to complicate the conversation for the sake of richer inquiry and broader understanding.

Some players can and do choose pacifism as an effective play-through strategy for video games, from the Looking Glass Studio's "first-person sneaker" *Thief: The Dark Project* (1998) to Ion Storm's CRPG *Deus Ex* (2000) to *Skyrim.* In *Skyrim,* for example, a player-character named Felix the Peaceful Monk publicly broadcasts his nonviolent pilgrimage through Tamriel, documenting his journey in a series of YouTube videos (Mullins 2011). Felix sneaks around a lot, avoiding conflict when possible. He only accepts quests that do not require violence. He calms or frightens opponents into retreat. Blogger Drew Dixon (2012), however, posits that while pacifism "generally works in real life," it can fall short as a gameplay strategy. He argues that gameplay pacifism in *Skyrim* "is neither virtuous nor immersive." Nevertheless, Dixon celebrates Felix the Peaceful Monk's resistance of a naïveté toward violence, widespread among video games designers and players. In a tangentially related discussion, Alexander Galloway (2006) expresses hope that video game artists will create "alternative algorithms" by designing "new grammars of action, not just new grammars of visuality" for gameplay (p. 125). Put another way, Galloway hopes that the domination of command-and-control protocols will gradually make room for "countergaming" proposals. As players resist the procedural logic of the CRPG, perhaps subversive new grammars will emerge from below.

The meaning of video gameplay exceeds that of violence alone, despite the implicit curriculum of militarism within many popular procedural designs. For example, video games can usher the player into an encounter with transcendence, an argument that this writer outlines elsewhere (Hayse 2009; 2011; 2012; forthcoming). Video gameplay can thrust the player into a revelatory encounter with the veiled Other. Some visitors to video game virtual realities take that journey because they long to discover something *more*. Michael Heim (1993) suggests that "In the face of the infinity of possible, virtual worlds," virtual reality sets the stage for "an experience of the sublime or awesome" (p. 137). On the other hand, Heim contends, those visitors must also bear the burden of digital finitude (p. 105-107). They know that computer-generated worlds are both limited and limiting. The computer readily lends itself to the limiting gameplay of violence and domination. Some players are content to be killers as Richard Bartle (1996) asserts. On the other hand, Bartle notes that other players enjoy gameplay for the sake of exploration and discovery. Players reflect a diverse range of gameplay affections and *Elder Scrolls* players are no exception.

The upcoming launch of *The Elder Scrolls Online* will provide additional insight into the question of violence and gameplay. What difference--if any--will the MMO (massively multiplayer online) setting make to the ES gameplay experience? As Don Ihde (1979) puts it, what aspects of gameplay will the ES MMO "amplify" and "reduce"? Will violence dominate the landscape of daily, online life, or will gentler pursuits, such as those found in *The Elder Scrolls V: Hearthfire* (2012) win the day? As an expansion to *Skyrim*, *Hearthfire Hearthfire* elicits the decidedly nonviolent gameplay of domesticity: building and furnishing a homestead, hiring a household staff and adopting and raising children. Are these gameplay elements sufficient to establish a widespread moral norm in Tamriel, or will barbarism and looting prevail? Clear foresight often eludes even the most prophetic critic, but history tells a cautionary tale in answer to this question. Richard Garriott's *Ultima* series was *The Elder Scrolls* of its day. The series began with *Akalabeth: World of Doom* (1980 California Pacific Computer), a traditional "hack and slash" CRPG.

Not long after, *Ultima IV: Quest of the Avatar* (1985 ORIGIN Systems) popularized ethical CRPG design with a moral compass embedded in the *Ultima IV*'s procedures. By the time of *Ultima VII: The Black Gate's* (1992 ORIGIN Systems) release, the world of Britannia stood above all others as the apex of "sandbox" gameplay--an open world of gameplay "freedom." When the MMO CRPG *Ultima Online* launched (Electronic Arts 1997) a few years later, industry leaders and players alike hoped that a digital utopia of craftsmanship, goodwill and virtue would emerge. Instead, chaos quickly erupted as journalist Amy Jo Kim (1998) explains:

Far from a place where virtue is rewarded, the kingdom (of Britannia) is ruled by intimidation, power dynamics, and conspicuous consumption. PKing (player-killing) to acquire worldly goods is the most lucrative career choice around. But that's not all. Denizens who live in accordance with the Eight Virtues often find themselves not only poor, bored, and frustrated, but inadvertently punished by the laws of the land. These high-minded players toil in small-time professions, while players with highly developed combat skills reign supreme: They terrorize newcomers, kill for money, and broadcast their wealth and power by building huge castles. It's a tough place to be a noble avatar.

Critics, theorists and players were shocked to see the rapid erosion of *Ultima's* social, ethical and aesthetic vision. Instead of building families and baking bread, Britannia's citizens were slaughtering the weak and devouring each other. Who can foresee the results when MMOs attempt to translate a mechanistic economy of rules and procedures into an organic ecology (Hayse 2009, p. 140n) of live player interactions and real-time social politics? The ES series promises a new degree of freedom to its online players, yet it lies nested within a procedural logic that readily recalls its military origins. In *The Elder Scrolls Online*, will the *imago Dei* of interdependence and intimacy transform Tamriel into a virtual kingdom of heaven or will the original sins of pride and violence corrupt and collapse this online world?

REFERENCE LIST

Bartle, R. (1996). Hearts, Clubs, Diamonds, Spades: Players Who Suit MUDs. *Journal of MUD Research, 1*(1). Retrieved from http://www.mud.co.uk/richard/hcds.htm

Barton, M. (2008). *Dungeons and desktops: the history of computer role-playing games*. Wellesley, MA: A. K. Peters.

Bogost, I. (2006). *Unit operations: an approach to videogame criticism*. Cambridge, MA: The MIT Press.

_____. (2007). *Persuasive games: the expressive power of videogames*. Cambridge, MA: The MIT Press.

Crogan, P. (2011). *Gameplay mode: war, simulation, and technoculture*. Minneapolis, MN: University of Minnesota Press.

Cuban, L. (1995). The Hidden Variable: How Organizations Influence Teacher Responses to Secondary Science Curriculum Reform. *Theory into Practice, 34*(1), 4-11.

Deterding, S. (2010). Living Room Wars: Remediation, Boardgames, and the Early History of Video Wargaming. In Nina B. Huntemann & Matthew Thomas Payne (Ed.), *Joystick soldiers: the politics of play in military video games*, (pp. 21-38). New York, NY: Routledge.

Dixon, D. (2012). The idealistic world of videogame pacifists [Web log]. Retrieved from http://gamechurch.com/the-idealistic-world-of-videogame-pacifists/

Donovan, T. (2010). *Replay: the history of video games*. Lewes, East Sussex: Yellow Ant.

Frasca, G. (2004). Videogames of the Oppressed: Critical Thinking,

Education, Tolerance, and Other Trivial Issues. In Noah Wardrip-Fruin & Pat Harrigan (Ed.), *First person: new media as story, performance, and game,* (pp. 85-94). Cambridge, MA: The MIT Press.

Galloway, A. (2006). *Gaming: essays on algorithmic culture.* Minneapolis, MN: University of Minnesota Press.

Gee, J. P. (2007). *What video games have to teach us about learning and literacy.* Revised and updated version. New York, NY: Palgrave Macmillan.

Giroux, H. A., and P. L. McLaren. (1992). Towards a Critical Pedagogy of Representation. In James Schwoch, Mimi White, & Susan Reilly (Ed.), *Media knowledge: readings in popular culture, pedagogy, and critical citizenship,* (pp. xv-xxxiv). Albany, NY: State University of New York Press.

Goodlad, J. I. (2004). *A Place Called School.* 2nd edition. New York, NY: McGraw-Hill.

Gorman, M. J. (2001). *Cruciformity: Paul's narrative spirituality of the cross.* Grand Rapids, MI: Eerdmans.

Greene, M. (1983). Introduction. In Henry Giroux & David Purpel (Ed.), *The hidden curriculum and moral education: Deception or discovery?,* (pp. 1-5). Berkeley, CA: McCutchan Publishing Corporation.

Halter, E. (2006). *From Sun Tzu to Xbox: war and video games.* New York, NY: Thunder's Mouth Press.

Hayse, M. (2011). The Mediation of Transcendence within the Legend of Zelda: The Wind Waker. In Jonathan L. Walls (Ed.), *The Legend of Zelda and Theology,* (pp. 83-96). Los Angeles, CA: Gray Matter Books.

_____. (2012). Spirituality. In Mark J. P. Wolf (Ed.), *Encyclopedia of Video Games: The Culture, Technology, and Art of Gaming,* (pp. 616-620). Santa Barbara, CA: Greenwood.

_____. (forthcoming). Transcendence. In Bernard Perron and Mark J. P. Wolf (Ed.), *The Routledge Companion to Video Game Studies.* New York, NY: Routledge.

Hayse, M. A. (2009). *Religious architecture in videogames: perspectives from curriculum theory and religious education.* (Unpublished doctoral dissertation). Trinity Evangelical Divinity School, Deerfield, IL.

Ihde, D. (1979). *Technics and praxis.* Dordrecht, Holland: D. Reidel.

Jackson, P. W. (1968). *Life in classrooms.* New York, NY: Holt, Rinehart, and Winston.

Kim, A. J. (1998). Killers Have More Fun. *Wired,* 6(05). Retrieved from http://www.wired.com/wired/archive/6.05/ultima.html

Lawrence, J. S. and R. Jewett. (2002). *The myth of the American superhero.* Grand Rapids, MI: Eerdmans.

Lenoir, T. (2000). All But War Is Simulation: The Military-Entertainment Complex. *Configurations, 8,* 289-435.

Lessig, L. (2006). *Code: and other laws of cyberspace, version 2.0.* New York, NY: Basic Books.

Meighan, R. (1981). *A sociology of educating.* London: Holt.

Mullins, D. (2011, December 5). Felix the peaceful monk #1 - good guy Felix [Video file]. Retrieved from http://www.youtube.com/watch?v=y2d2KRIUYCM

Pinar, W. F. (2011). *What is curriculum theory?* 2nd edition. New York, NY: Routledge.

Pinar, W. F., Reynolds, W. M., Slattery, P., and Taubman, P. M. (2006). *Understanding curriculum: an introduction to the study of historical and contemporary curriculum discourses.* 5th edition. New York, NY: Peter Lang.

Slattery, P. (2013). *Curriculum development in the postmodern era.* 3rd edition. New York, NY: Routledge.

Snyder, B. R. (1973). *The hidden curriculum.* Cambridge, MA: The MIT Press.

Squire, K. (2011). *Video games and learning: teaching and participatory culture in the digital age.* New York, NY: Teachers College Press. Toles,

T. (1985). Video Games and Military Ideology. *Arena Review,* 9(3), 58-76.

Toles, T. (1985). Video Games and Military Ideology. *Arena Review,* 9(3), 58-76.

Wells, H. G. ([1911] 2006). *Floor games.* Alexandria, VA: Skirmisher Publishing.

_____. ([1913] 2004). *Little wars: a game for boys from twelve years of age to one hundred and fifty and for that more intelligent sort of girls who like boys' games and books.* Alexandria, VA: Skirmisher Publishing.

Wink, W. (1992). *Engaging the powers: discernment and resistance in a world of domination.* Minneapolis: Augsburg Fortress.

Endnotes

[1] Special thanks to Nathan Brumet and Benjamin Oney for sharing their thoughtful Elder Scrolls insights with me during the writing of this essay. Their critical perspectives helped to clarify my own thinking.

ONTOLOGICAL FRAMEWORKS:

A New Technological Vocabulary for Doctrine[1]

BY JOSHUA WISE

The days of nearly ubiquitous Greek philosophical education are gone. It has been said that in the second century, if you were a Roman or Greek, when you woke up in the morning, stepped outside and saw the sky, you did so as a Middle Platonist.[2] Such a Platonist would have readily understood, if not the substance of the Nicene Creed, at least the general world of its categories. It now requires students receive years of philosophical, historical, and theological training to achieve a familiarity with the concepts and terminologies of the early Church debates. We cannot expect the generally educated churchgoer to understand the concept of a hypostasis. In fact, experience shows that we cannot expect many trained theologians to really understand it.

We have lost, in a significant way, the common context for understanding some of our most foundational statements as Christians. If we observe that this presents a problem for Christianity, then three possible courses of action present themselves as responses. The first would be to do nothing, and to effectively declare that the problem is not worth solving, or at least not at this point. The second would be to attempt to reeducate the general church population in the worldviews of the early church so that their concepts might be at least approximated in the contemporary setting in order so we might understand (approximately) the meanings of the normative statements of faith that they produced.

The third option is for those who have done the work to understand the original concepts, to look for common experience and conception from which to draw a new vocabulary that may be helpful in clarifying the faith. In this way, connections could be made with locations of meaning for the contemporary church that explain of the central meanings of the original statements of faith.

This approach seems most appropriate for the following reasons. First, it is a method that is essentially modular. If we conceive of the process of communicating the meaning of the church's statements as involving the following elements: Meaning, statement, translation, audience, and understanding, this approach considers as generally stable the meaning and statement of Christian Doctrine, while acknowledging that the audience and their understanding is ever changing.[3] Upon examining the audience and their understanding, the appropriate translation can be selected to communicate the meaning of the statement. This modular approach allows for both the permanence and normative elements of the original statement and meaning, while not assigning this status to the interpretive/translation element.

Secondly, this approach that at least attempts to be faithful to the method of the creation of the normative statements of faith that are being translated into the contemporary culture. It is the meaning of the creeds and general theology of the body of Christ that is pointed to by these expressions. The meaning is, however, communicated by the language, culture, and conceptions of the day. Therefore, a thoroughly situated and contextualized interpretation acknowledges both the fact that this method is inherent to how humanity naturally communicates meaning, and the fact that the church has sanctified this process by expressing divine revelation through it.

Thirdly, it attempts to emulate the process as it is first sanctified by the divine self revelation in the life of Israel; first through the Torah, Writings and Prophets, and then through the Incarnate Word who drew on the world around Him for images of the Kingdom of God. It is in the spirit of the Incarnate Word that this method seeks to translate larger realities into smaller ones. In our particular example, the relationship of the divine to the creation by means of virtual worlds.

A difficulty, however, also presents itself in the use of this method. The translation of a text's meaning assumes that the person translating understands the meaning of the original text. This assumes some level of translation has already occurred, at least to some group of people who undertake the work of translating the meaning to larger bodies. What occurs then is a translation of a translation. This essay does not attempt to address this particular problem, but simply to outfit those who seek a more contemporary reality with which to relate the doctrines of Christianity. Our proposed theory is conceptual and is intended to be used as a demonstrable model or testing ground, much the same way that angels were used in the middle ages. We may still live in a world shot through with angelic light, but our culture is far more comfortable with Pac-Man and Super Mario Brothers than it is with the Heavenly Host. So it is to them we turn to conceptualize our world.

Thus, we will use the concept of the computer-simulated worlds of gaming to examine the idea of the Ontological Framework.

ONTOLOGICAL FRAMEWORK:

A Definition

To discuss our topic we first must establish a number of terms that we will use throughout this essay. The first, *Ontological Framework*, is our focal point. A framework is, by definition, a structure or enclosure for containing something other than itself. Our term, Ontological Framework, is meant to represent a structure of being that is self-contained.[4] Any entity within an Ontological Framework (OFW) shares, at its base, the same level of being as every other entity in the same framework. Thus, every entity in a framework shares with every other entity in a framework potential mutual causality and conditioning. Thus all entities in the framework may *potentially* influence each other in being and state. *Entity* here means any existent within a framework.[5] The potential mutual causality and conditioning of entities in an OFW is conditioned by the rules of that framework, or its *laws*. The laws function in two ways to condition this potential mutual causality and conditioning. First, they dictate what kinds of Entities may exist in the OFW. Second, they define how different Entities may interact with each other.

Any two Entities that do not have potential mutual causality or conditioning, as conditioned by the laws of the OFW, are not part of the same OFW. Thus, unless two Entities could affect each other, given different attributes or circumstances, or even different laws, they are not part of the same framework. For example, by our current understanding of physics, two objects traveling away from each other at the speed of light, unless both are turned once more toward each other, have no possibility of affecting each other. If they continue on indefinitely in those directions, they will not have any ability to condition each other. However, if we simply adjust their attributes, speed, location, direction, we find that they could easily condition each other and are, thus, in the same OFW.

We might not say the same about a writer at Bethesda and a character in *Daggerfall.* The character exists (at least conceptually) in the fictional world of the play. If we move the character from one location to another, or change his race, gender, age or even temporal location in the story, he is no more able to directly affect the writer than previously. If we remove him from his game and put him into our world, we have changed his framework, but not any of his attributes. He has stopped being an entity in one framework and become an entity in the other.[6]

RELATIONAL FRAMEWORKS

If we accept these descriptors and limitations for what we mean by an OFW, we begin to see how OFWs might relate to each other. Central to the idea of relationality is context. I take it as a tautology that no two things may have relationship with each other without some kind of shared context. In other words, no relation is possible without a medium of relation. Without a medium of relation to condition the kind of relation, two things may not have a relationship with each other.

Therefore, if we speak of the relationships of OFWs, it must be done with an eye toward the idea of an accessible mutual context. This essay proposes two basic relationship pairs, one asymmetrical and one symmetrical, that can exist between OFWs. The first is the foundational/dependent relationship. The second is the relationship between two or more frameworks equally dependent on the same foundational framework.

The foundational/dependent relationship is one in which the *Dependent OFW* is one that exists wholly because of the *Foundational OFW.* The context or medium of relationship is, in this case, the foundational OFW itself. The relationship is explicable and possible because of the Foundational OFW and exists as a result of the Foundational OFW. This is, of course, an asymmetrical relationship, as an OFW cannot be dependent upon an OFW that is wholly dependent on it for its own being.

The relationship involving two or more Dependent OFWs equally wholly dependent on shared Foundational OFWs has for its medium of relationship the mutually shared Foundational OFW. This relationship can be highly complex as it may involve many levels of parallel Foundational/Dependent OFWs in relationship to each other. To understand the ramifications of these complex relationships, we turn to some basic observations and conclusions about these relationships.

ATTRIBUTES OF RELATIONSHIPS

Here we will lay out a number of different attributes of the two basic relationship types described above. These attributes will show how OFWs exist and interact with each other, presumably regardless of the laws of each particular OFW. These attributes are derived from observation of these relationships as they exist in our world and as may be deduced logically from the proposed structures.

1. Due to the fact that the Foundational/Dependent relationship of OFWs is described as the dependent OFW relying fully on the Foundational OFW, we may observe that the Foundational OFW has the potential for total control over the Dependent OFW. This is due to the fact that there is no aspect of the Dependent OFW that does not find its origin or being in the Foundational OFW. However, the control is only potential as it is conditioned by the rules and entities of the two OFWs.

Thus any element of any game on my computer is fully accessible to our world. However, due to the rules of our world and how the computer code is written, that access is limited in practice. Unless there are controls for each and every element made available to me as the player, there may be things that I simply cannot change in the game. As well, someone who is a hundred miles away cannot change anything about the game directly.

2. Entities in the Dependent OFW are non-identical Entities in the foundational OFW. An Entity in the Dependent OFW, because it is fully dependent on the Foundational OFW, exists within the Foundational Framework as one or more Entities. However, it is not the same kind of Entity in both frameworks. They may be analogously the same, but not identically the same.[7] An entity in a Dependent Framework that is identical with its entity in the foundational framework ceases to be an entity in the dependent framework. The test of this is the question of potential mutual causality and conditioning, which we observe in attribute 3.

3. Entities in a Dependent OFW are observed to be Entities in their own framework because they do not have mutual potential causality/conditioning in the Foundational OFW in their identity as entities in the Dependent OFW. However, the Entities in the Foundational OFW, though comprising the Entities of the Dependent OFW, retain their mutual causal and conditioning status with other Entities in the Foundational OFW. Entities within the Foundational OFW that do not comprise the Dependent OFW may have causality and conditioning over the Dependent OFW, but only by means of the Entities that comprise the Dependent OFW to which they are in relation by means of their mutually shared OFW.

4. It is also observable that events or actions within the Dependent OFW are non-identical events or actions in the Foundational

OFW and vice-versa. The change of status of an entity in a Dependent OFW necessitates an asymmetrical change of status in the Foundational OFW. The change of status in an Entity comprising the Dependent OFW may or may not necessitate an asymmetrical change of status in the Dependent OFW. It will necessitate a change if the state change is a controlling factor in the composition of the Dependent OFW's Entity. It will not if the state change is not a controlling factor in the composition of the Dependent OFW's Entity.

For example, the change of size to a virtual object does not depend on an equal change of size in the hardware and software that generates it. Instead, an asymmetrical change, the change of state of energy or transistors, brings about the change in the virtual object's size. However, there are changes to the computer running the program and all of its components, which need not bring about changes in the virtual world, such as the position of the computer in our world.

5. Any causality or conditioning between two or more Dependent OFWs that share the same Foundational OFW is accomplished through the medium of a mutual Foundational OFW. This is true no matter how far down a tree of Foundational/Dependent frameworks a system goes.

6. The kind of relationship between Foundational and Dependent OFW is defined purely by the Foundational OFW.

7. Because Entities are defined by the Laws of their particular OFW, entities in two or more different OFWs either may be of the same kind or only analogously of the same kind.

A DEPENDENT FRAMEWORK:

Skyrim

Given the abstract nature of the above statements, it is useful to consider a test case for our study. Here, we will use the game *The Elder Scrolls V: Skyrim* as our considered dependent framework. This will allow us to test and demonstrate the nature of the attributes we have observed. However, before we begin, we must disentangle some of the complications of using such an example. To do this, we must distinguish between four specific realities that refer to *Skyrim*.

Four Referents for a Conceptual World

1. Hardware/Software/Material Reality: The state of any computer program on a conventional computer is, at its base, simply a configuration of matter and energy, like any object in our world.[8] In this way, they are indistinguishable from any other object or configuration of energy and matter. A simple examination of the configuration of subatomic particles, atoms and molecules would not present anything identifiable as a computer program. It is only in the larger structure of the computer hardware, a processor, memory, hard-drive, etc, that any computer program begins to be knowable as such. The many layers of programs that function at any given time on a piece of hardware exist only as programs in the context of a system that is designed to support them. We may call these systems "emergent" in the sense that they are systems built from basic components that construct sub-systems. By emergent, however, we do not mean to suggest that they come about by the simple process of nature. As far as we can

tell, it requires rational minds to create the systems we see as computers and their programs.

This level of the computer program is very important to our understanding of the relationship between our own world and dependent OFWs to which our world is Foundational. Ultimately, all changes that take place in the dependent OFWs take place at the lowest level of our own reality. However, they are identifiable most easily at the level of the computer hardware. The change of state of a cluster of transistors in our world reflects the lateral movement of an object in two dimensional space in a game.

Therefore, we will reference this first level of the computer program as the *Material Reality* of the Dependent OFW. It is the Material Reality of the Dependent OFW in our own world which we can affect directly by the application of electricity, hammers or water. A virtual world can be handily destroyed by a swift kick to the computer's processor.

2. The Fictional World: This is often linked to a virtual world in a way that does not, in fact, affect its reality as a Dependent OFW. When we consider *The Elder Scrolls* as a whole, we are considering a world of incredibly rich and complex fiction. We encounter myth, history, personalities, locations and artifacts. There are books with text that relate many of these things to us in the game itself, as well as in our own world (very much like the book you're holding now). The fiction is often the reason people are enthralled by the world of *The Elder Scrolls*. However, when we speak of *The Elder Scrolls*

as a Dependent OFW, we very specifically do not mean this aspect of the world.

Our understanding of a dependent OFW here is concerned with Entities that exist in relationship to each other conditioned by each other, but also conditioned by their attributes. A Dwemer warrior is identifiable by the attributes of that particular entity in our understanding of an OFW. Those attributes are meaningful only in how they affect the entity's being and attributes in relation to other Entities in the OFW. The fiction related to the Entity is not a meaningful attribute of any Entity in a game of *The Elder Scrolls*, or really any game. Only because the fiction is reflected in the actual attributes of the entities is the fiction part of what we call the OFW. Yet even these attributes are distinct from the fiction, and theoretically only accidentally or loosely related to the fiction, for they could be otherwise. It would be a poor game, but not a logical contradiction, if the main character of *Morrowind* was described as a female Nord in the fiction, but the game allowed the player to choose whatever gender and race she desired. Such an inconsistency is possible due to the loose relationship of the fiction to the actual OFW.

Therefore, while this may be the most interesting level of the world with which the rest of this book engages, it is not, in fact, a very meaningful definition for our theory here.[9]

3. The Mental World: By the *Mental World* is that construct of the world of *The Elder Scrolls* which exists in our minds. It is what I mean when I say *The Elder Scrolls*, and will be somewhat different than what Joshua Gonnerman means in his essay. It includes my experiences of playing the games, the

experience of my character finding amazing artifacts in the ancestral tombs of a tribal people in the game *Morrowind*. It is made up of images, bits of history, theology and characters. It is The Elder Scrolls as it exists in my own mind, but not as it exists in the fiction in total, as the Fictional World does.

Such a construct of the world links together different play sessions, the reading of text outside of the world, as well as related information that I might read on a news site about the series. It even, to a lesser degree, involves my interactions with people who work at Bethesda. It is a complex structure infused with emotions and meaning.

This also is not what we mean here when we refer to the OFW of The Elder Scrolls. This quasi-persistent relation of thoughts in my own mind, while related to the Dependent OFW, is distinct from it. Its constituent components exist in the same world as my apartment, or the computer on which I'm writing this. They do not exist on the same level as the actual Entities in the world of *The Elder Scrolls*. However, this Mental World will be important when we consider the concept of meaning in an OFW.

4. The Virtualized World: By the Virtualized World, we mean precisely the virtualized environment that emerges when a program is run on a computer. In the case of *The Elder Scrolls* it is any particular "play session" of the game that has a definitive beginning point in time and has a potential ending point at a later time. When the Entities of the game enter the memory of the computer and begin to relate to each other by the rules defined by the game's systems, the OFW comes

into being. When they cease to meet these requirements, the OFW no longer exists.[10]

Thus, any two play sessions of a game in *The Elder Scrolls*, are their own Dependent OFW's. They relate to each other only by means of sharing in a common Foundational OFW and as related in our minds by means of the Fictional World and the Abstract World. In our world they are related to each other in the same way that all Entities are related to each other, by space and time.

The virtualized world then is our primary meaning of the OFW in this text. It is with this which the player interacts through her input devices of keyboard and mouse, gamepad or other user interface devices. It is this world that is visually represented to the player through the graphical and audio layer that exists within our own OFW and which must be distinguished from this visual and audible representation. Entities in the Dependent OFW of a play-session of the *Oblivion*, for example, are not "Altmer" and "Khajiit." They are not dark skinned, light skinned, or of a particular hair color. Instead, these attributes, which are attributes readable and assignable by the system of the game, are presented to the player through the two-dimensional image of a virtual three dimensional representation. Yet that representation, created to exist within our OFW so that it can be directly observed, is merely a loosely related abstraction of the realities of the OFW itself. Just as with the example of the main character of *Morrowind* above in the Fictional World description, the visual representation of the world is only loosely linked to the Dependent OFW in itself. A player may assign the attribute "black hair" to her character, but the game might just as easily show red or blue hair without any affect on how the OFW itself interprets the way in which Entities and Laws work together with that attribute.

Thus, we must think of the Virtualized World purely in terms of Entities, Events and Laws. The laws of the program determine which kinds of Entities can exist in the world, and how those entities interact given their existence, states and Events. The Events of the world determine which Entities exist and their states. The Entities interact through Events conditioned by the Laws of the world.

Abstracting out then the Fictional and Mental Worlds, we may observe that when a character walks through a town in *Skyrim*, what is actually happening in the OFW is that the state of the Entity which is of the class "Character,"[11] is undergoing state changes in location attributes (probably defined in an x,y,z coordinate system). No real "movement" is going on, or if we say that there is real movement, we must say that it is only analogous.[12] The laws of the game determine which other Entities this character can interact with and what kinds of interactions can be had.

Given this explanation of the Virtualized World, we now go on to test the attributes listed above to this OFW to show how they derive from and cohere in such a model as this.

Testing the Attributes
of Relationship

Here we will consider how our world (the Foundational OFW) relates to the world of *The Elder Scrolls* (the Dependent OFW), and how any sibling relations of the Dependent OFWs might relate to each other. We will test each of the Attributes of Relationship that we have laid out above.

1. Total control of the dependent OFW should be obvious. There is nothing in an instance of a running game that is not accessible to our reality. This should not be confused, however, with the accessibility of any particular element of the game with any particular Entity in our world. A theoretical Martian should not be thought to have access to the day/night cycle of my play-session. In fact, only through the console commands of the game do I have access to this element. This is because the potential for control of every element of the Dependent OFW is necessary, but the actual control is conditioned by the configuration of our own reality. The computer running the program has access to all of the elements of game (otherwise they would not exist). However, that does not mean that any other Entity in our world necessarily does.

2. Entities in *The Elder Scrolls* exist as Entities of their own type in that OFW, but also exist as collections of states of Entities in relation to each other in our OFW. Thus, while a character might be of the type "Character" in *The Elder Scrolls*, it exists as an array of Entities which are not the type "character", but are instead of the type "transistor," electron, etc. in a computer. Furthermore, a character in our world is

not capable of being a character in that world. This may not be absolutely true for all possible Foundational/Dependent OFW relationships. However, even if it were possible, the character in our world would have to be of the same type only analogously in the Dependent OFW, as the two types of characters exist in different relationships and frameworks.

3. The Entities in an instance of a game of *Skyrim* are part of their own OFW precisely because, as the entities themselves, they do not have mutual potential causality or conditioning over Entities in our own world. A magical artifact in the world of *The Elder Scrolls* may have many attributes that affect the other Entities in its own world. Yet, as the magical artifact, it has a far more limited ability to impact our world. In fact, it can only affect our world by its representation in our world, which we have determined is not, in fact, the same thing as the entity itself.

    However, the Entities in our own OFW that make up the magical artifact in the Dependent OFW remain Entities in our own OFW that can be affected in all of the normal ways in which they could be, even if they were not bringing about an OFW. Thus, there is potential causality from our OFW to the Dependent OFW by way of affecting the elements that make up the Dependent OFW. However, it is easily observable that this is not mutual. The Entity in the Dependent OFW cannot get at the constituent elements of the entities in our OFW. In other words, no matter how powerful a flaming sword is in *The Elder Scrolls*, it cannot cut the simple wooden chair across from me. But that wooden chair can smash the computer I'm working on and wipe the sword out of existence. Or, to put it another way, a character in Arena may have a terrible allergy to feathers. However, prod as I might at my laptop with a down comforter, the character is unaffected.

4. As stated earlier, the movement of a character in *The Elder Scrolls*, which is described as directional or locational movement, involves an asymmetrical change in our world. While the character may "move" a hundred "yards" in his world, the Entities which make up the character do not in fact move a hundred yards in our world. They change in state in an asymmetrical way. A planet-sized object moving across the galaxy in the virtual world involves some very minute changes in our own. As well, very minute changes in our world bring about asymmetrical changes in the virtual world. A series of zeroes and ones change and a character goes from dead to alive.

5. When we see how two games of *Redguard* might affect each other, it becomes clear that the relations of two or more OFWs equally dependent on the same Foundational OFW are as they are described in the attribute. They cannot, by definition, directly affect each other, otherwise they would not be distinct instances of the game. Instead, any interaction must be accomplished through their Foundational OFW, our world. This could be imagined in a number of different ways. A third program running on a computer that is running both programs may be watching for changes in one program to feed data into the second. A player playing the first might

give information he discovered to another player who then uses it in her game. Even a player throwing up their hands in victory at one computer might accidentally bump another player who erroneously inputs a command into his game. But the sword in one game cannot cut the ogre in the other.[13]

This, of course, works even if we imagine *that The Elder Scrolls XXV* will be complex enough to host a game of *Daggerfall* running in its own world. The Entities of *Daggerfall* could only affect our world by first affecting the entities of its own parent OFW (*Elder Scrolls XXV*), which would then affect our world. Only then, could the effects be transmitted into another instance of the game running somewhere else.

6. The relationship between our world and the dependent OFWs that our world hosts is defined entirely by our world. The dependent OFWs are what they are and can be what they can be, only because of the nature of our own OFW. By the configuration of Entities, Laws and Events, our OFW can host particular kinds of Dependent OFWs. Given that our OFW is a construct of matter/energy, and in dimensional space-time, our relationship to the Dependent OFWs is defined by these elements. However, that does not mean that the relationship between any individual Entity in our OFW is materially or spatially related to any entity in the hosted OFW. Instead, those relationships exist, as shown in points 3 and 4, with the Entities in our world which constitute the Entities in their OFW. But the chair in which I am sitting does not have a spatial relationship with a chain in an inn in any of the cities of *Morrowind*.

Understanding this distinction, we maintain that the relationship between a Foundational OFW and the Dependent OFW is defined entirely by the Foundational OFW. We make Dependent OFWs by configuring matter and energy to bring about sustained OFWs because our reality is configured in such a way as to allow this to happen. Other kinds of OFWs would not bring about Dependent OFWs in this way if they are not configured in the same way as our own.

By an examination then of these principles, we can seen how a single Ontological Framework functions in relationships to other Frameworks. We then will use these attributes to consider now a number of Christian theological areas. It is not the intention of this essay to exhaust these topics in light of the theory of Ontological Frameworks, but instead to simply propose starting points and considerations for further theological reflection.

THEOLOGICAL STARTING POINTS

The model for Creation

Perhaps the most obviously relevant question that this theory addresses is the theory of Creation Ex Nihilo, which has been central to Christianity since its debates with Neoplatonism. The Christian doctrine, as it is traditionally expressed, is that God, in creating the universe, did not use any prior existent or substance. In distinction from human creation, which merely rearranges existing matter in an existing space, God did not use anything that pre-existed its being as what we know as the universe.[14]

The above paragraph intentionally avoids the word "nothing", which has been a difficult one for both theologians and non-theologians alike.[15]

Instead, let us negate not the "thing" but the pre-existence of all things in a creation. God makes that which God simply commands to come into being. This is true of the existent which is called into being and the context for the existent. It would be nonsense to think of God calling a planet into being without the planet, which by definition is three dimensional, having a three-dimensional environment in which to exist.

Our creation, then, is one which God calls into being, matter, energy, space, time, all "at once."[16] The whole system comes into being and the entities within the system begin to act according to the laws of the system.[17]

This relationship of Creator to creation, when considered in the light of the attributes proposed in this theory, holds to the traditional Christian doctrines. The creation is defined purely in the terms of the Creator. It exists by sharing in some way in God's existence. It is good because it shares in God's goodness. It is free because it shares in God's freedom. Parts of it are rational because they share in God's thought.[18]

As well, the limitations of that participation are evident. Our being is less than God's being, our goodness less than God's. We are derived, God is original. The same must be said of our prime example of *The Elder Scrolls*. Morrowind is a less real land than Wisconsin, because Morrowind participates in, and is dependent on the world in which Wisconsin exists. To remove Morrowind is not to remove the world which has Wisconsin in it. But to remove the world where Madison, WI exists is to wipe out Morrowind.

We then see that the traditional doctrines of creation match up quite well with the theory proposed here. Understanding that the foundational OFW (God) determines the relationship between the Foundational OFW and the Dependent OFW, prevents us from falling into a kind of Neo-platonic emanation. The free God freely creates our world and defines the relationship by that freedom. We are saved from potential emanation due to the simplicity and unconditioned nature of God. Since God does not exist in an environment that is distinct from God and does not obey external laws that would dictate how God relates to other things, the whole OFW of God is God in Godself. Thus the unified and simple reality of the Freedom of God (God) and the Power of God (God) by which God creates is the source and descriptor of the relationship between God and creation. As Karl Rahner has written:

> *The difference between God and the world is of such a nature that God establishes and is the difference of the world from himself, and for this reason he establishes the closest unity precisely in the differentiation. For if the difference itself comes from God, and, if we can put it his way, is itself identical with God, then the difference between God and the world is to be understood quite differently than the difference between categorical realities.* [19]

Considering then that our theory here is in keeping with the traditional expression of the orthodox doctrine of Creation Ex Nihilo, we now will consider several ramifications for this theory in current discussion areas in theology.

Science and the Supernatural

The modern dialog with science has revealed a gap in the understanding between generally understood concepts of God and the traditional understanding of how God interacts with the universe. Significant objections have been raised about the fittingness of a God who sets up a system and then interferes with it. A God who is all knowing and all powerful would not need to interfere with a perfect creation due to the fact that the machine could simply be set up perfectly to act as it should. As well, interference from the "outside" seems to raise two problems. First, the laws of nature would, being suspended, create an erratic world not conducive to predictability. Second, a God who interfered with the laws set up would seem to be breaking His own laws.

The first question is not one with which we will deal directly here, but is better considered in a discussion of time and eternity. The second and third, however, are directly addressed by our theory.

Taking our model of *The Elder Scrolls* as an example of a dependent OFW, we must ask whether or not our interaction with the world, which must be by definition "supernatural" to that world, in fact, makes the laws of the world erratic.[20] Second, we must ask whether or not that interaction "breaks the laws" of the world.

It seems obvious that regular interactions between our OFW and the Dependent OFW of a game of *Daggerfall* do not bring about erratic and unpredictable events. The introduction of the movement of a character or objects controlled directly by a player, does not introduce radically new or unpredictable behavior. Instead, the natural laws and Entities in the OFW absorb and deal with these events handily.[21] We move a sword, the physics of the world take hold of it and determine how the sword moves. We move a character and the character moves as it should. Things do not fall apart.

We do observe some level of problem when cheat codes are entered. We turn "no clipping" and move through walls. The game might crash or a quest might be bugged after the fact. However, as any programmer will tell you, this is because the program was not designed to take these particular movements into account. The system breaks because it is designed in a way such that it cannot account for these particular kinds of events. Our own universe is hardly the kind of universe that begins to fall apart if a dead body suddenly starts living again. We need not be concerned that the universe will "crash" if new events are entered into it, or if new states are given to matter or energy. The errors that we see when we begin to manipulate data in a virtual world are the errors that show the limitations of the simulation. They do not imply that our own universe is such that if God should introduce changes in particular situations, we should see corresponding "bugs" in the laws of physics.

Secondly, we can consider whether or not by interacting with the universe, God is breaking God's own rules. We can see pretty quickly that this is not the case when we interact with virtual worlds. The point of *The Elder Scrolls* is not that it should simply go on by itself alone as a simulation. Some worlds are built for that reason, but Arena was not. Instead, *Arena, Daggerfall*, etc. are built to be engaged by players. Their end, as it were, is to be interacted with. They are only complete when that which is supernatural to them is introduced. When the player moves the mouse and pushes the "W" key to go forward, the game is fulfilling its purpose in a way that it was not by simply running as a program. The dependent OFW was made for the purposes of the Foundational OFW. We might argue that this is not necessary, but it becomes hard to imagine a Foundational OFW bringing a Dependent OFW into existence for no reason. Even if that reason is merely to be observed, there is some point to the thing.

The main point here is that, far from "breaking the rules" of the Dependent OFW that Arena is, a player who introduces supernatural interaction into that world is fulfilling its purpose. Christianity has argued the same for God and our world from very early on. When we consider this ancient teaching with our own experience with virtual worlds, we see a striking similarity and congruity.

It seems then, that the application of our theory brings about two very interesting answers to modern problems. The introduction of activity by God into our nature need not bring about untrustworthy physical laws, and the introduction of activity by God need not contradict the purpose and integrity of the world itself.

The Laws of Physics

One of the ramifications of Attribute 1 is that the laws of a Dependent OFW are constructed in the terms of the Foundational OFW. They exist, not as Entities within the Dependant OFW, but as conditions in which the Dependent Entities exist. Therefore, they are observable in the Dependent OFW only as effects and not in themselves. An observant subjective Entity in a theoretical *Elder Scrolls* game of the future might be able to deduce many of the Laws that hold her world together. However, because the Laws themselves are written in terms of our world (code run on computers), and not her world, the medium in which her Laws are written is not accessible to her directly. Instead, only by experimentation, observation and repeated testing could she come to understand what the Laws are. We can see why she would not be able to have access to the Laws of her own world, since they are defined external to her own world.

It is interesting, then, that we find that science in our world is in the same situation. The failure of science to understand the "why" of the laws of physics has led some as publically visible as Stephen Hawking to declare that the question "why" is no longer valid.[22] Because the "why" of things is opaque to us, it is not considered by some to be a question that can be asked. If the OFW theory is correct, we can see why we would not be able to get at the laws of our own OFW, for they would (and must) exist in the terms of our Foundational OFW.

Now, it need not be that our immediate Foundational OFW be the naked will of God with no intervening realities in between. That may be the case, but it may not. But due to Attributes 1 and 2 above, Entities in our OFW are necessarily represented in every Foundational OFW above it, and thus are immediately the result of the will of God. Whatever is the highest Foundational OFW will have immediately for its laws the decrees of God that it should be an OFW with those exact laws. To understand, then, why the universe is as it is, God must be queried for answers. It is not that "why" is the wrong question, it has simply been asked of the wrong party.

Meaning

Much of the popular modern debate surrounding video games has centered around the meaning that we convey to them and that they convey to us. There has been concern regarding their effect on our perception of violence. However, underlying this is the question of how meaning works in a dependent OFW.

If we take purely for our definition of a video game like *The Elder Scrolls*, meanings 1 and 4, as we have been, we may quickly see that meaning has no place in the OFW. Meaning is a concept conveyed to and by subjective realities that have the potential to appreciate meaning conveyed to them. When I move a chair from one place to another in a room, I may be conveying meaning through this action to the person who will sit in it. The action has meaning to those subjective agents in the room. It has no meaning to the chair.

As objects exist in computer code or in relational systems that emerge from that code being run on a computer, they at this point can neither perceive meaning, nor convey it to each other. Nor, as Entities changing in states in relation to each other by a defined set of rules, can they have meaning for us. The change of a data state from False to True, or from 1024 to 2048, can have no substantial meaning for us at all except that it point to some other reality which we connect to it.

Thus we must bring in at least meaning 3 from above, though this nearly always involves bringing in meaning 2 as well. The fiction that I affix to the game represented to me, and the fiction that the creators mean for me to affix to those images and sounds, creates a layer of interpretation that allows me to imbue them with meaning and receive meaning from them. It is by the fiction and interpretation of the images I perceive that I find meaning in the changes of data states in the computer. It is within a realm of fiction, which is not inherent to the OFW itself, that I consider the actions of a character virtuous, dastardly or cowardly.[23] In the context of our own world, there are no ethical or unethical changes of data in a virtual world. It is only by their effects on our world that they become meaningful and ethical.[24]

As well, the meaning of actions in those worlds take on ethical dimensions insofar as they retain ethical dimensions in our own world. If I betray a friend in a multiplayer game, the action has no ethical meaning on the level of the OFW in which the action took place. There is, in itself, nothing unethical about the changes of state that take place within the game world, even in context.[25] However, the meaning of the action and the ethical ramifications exist on the level at which my friend and I exist. The dependent OFW has simply become the theater in which our ethical dilemma plays out.[26]

Thus, the ethical or meaningful elements of the Dependent OFW derive their ethics or meaning from the Foundational OFW.[27]

We may object, however, that if we were to create conscious beings in a dependent OFW and they were to come up with their own ethical or meaningful systems, that this observation would be belied. However, this is not so. While the subjective Entities in the virtual world might value their own systems of meaning or ethics, they would not be intrinsically meaningful or ethical, as they are ultimately grounded in non-meaningful and non-ethical realities in our own world. Only by deciding that they have real meaning or real ethical value can our OFW imbue them with meaning or value. The change of a data state, no matter how complex, is not itself valuable, meaningful or ethical, unless we first imbue it with those characteristics. Only by lending our own value to that system can it have value.

Once more, we find that the observed realities cleave closely to the traditional Christian teachings regarding meaning and morality. Only by God's decree and declaration does the world have ultimate meaning or moral character. Without this decree by the Foundational OFW, our ethics are merely relative and our meaning subjective. This does not deny that there can be ethics in a world that are not linked to a Foundational OFW, only that those ethics lack the weight and universal validity that they would otherwise have, if so linked.

Epistemology/Revelation

The question of epistemology that we have touched on lightly in the section on the laws of physics can be broadened to take in the whole question of knowledge within a Dependent OFW. Knowledge within a Dependent OFW of its Foundational OFW appears to be limited entirely to the terms of the Dependent OFW. A conscious subject in a Dependent OFW, if aware of the fact that it is in a Dependent OFW, appears only to be able to conceive of the Foundational OFW in the terms of the Dependent OFW.

Considering *The Elder Scrolls* as our example, if the Nerevarine were to become aware that the world in which he or she existed was a video game, he or she could not conceive of our world in any other terms than those which are present to him in his own world. Given that our world is three dimensional, and the world of *The Elder Scrolls* is at least analogously three dimensional, the Nerevarine could, at least, understand that we have height, weight, and how we move. But this would of course not be the case if we created a two-dimensional world[28] or a non-spatial world in which objects interact.[29] In fact, unless in the design of the subjective Entities in a virtual world, we decide that they should see their world in an analogous way to how we perceive it, we need not assume that even the Nerevarine would perceive his world in a three-dimensional way.[30]

But no matter how close the virtual world's rules are to our own, a subjective Entity will always understand our world in the terms of its own. This relates greatly to semiotics. Even if a conscious subject were given the idea of "standing" how it functioned within the virtual world would be distinct from how it would function in our world. The sounds and meaning behind "standing" would have their own particular meaning in the virtual world distinct from our own, as the actors who stand in that world do it differently than we do. In fact, only a truly analogous relationship can be established between any action in a Foundational OFW and a Dependent OFW.[31]

Ultimately then, any speech or thought by a conscious subject in a Dependent OFW must be either admittedly analogous or, ultimately, apophatic. One can imagine easily the first virtual philosopher who addresses her maker saying "I praise thee, Oh Harry, who is wise and knowing and exists beyond my wisdom and knowing. Or rather, I praise thee, Oh Harry who is beyond wisdom, and knowing, and even being!" And she would be right, at least as far as saying that whatever kind of wisdom or knowing or being that she has, Harry is beyond them.

It also seems interesting that the analogy appears, in fact, also to work in the other direction. We can speak of the events in a virtual world only in analogy. We may speak of the changes in our own world which constitute the changes in the virtual world in as close to direct language as we can (for much of our language about our own world is done in metaphor and analogy). However, when I say that a character in a game exists, I do not mean it in the same way that I mean it when I say that my wife exists. Nor do I mean it in the same way that I mean that God exists. However, the second comparison is most interesting. Our analogy for that which is Dependent to us is similar to the analogy to that which is Foundational to us. This seems to show that all knowledge in an OFW is restrained within that OFW by its own terminology. To communicate with a Dependent OFW, a Foundational OFW would need to do one of two things: Bring the Entity from the Dependent OFW into the Foundational OFW, or speak to the Entity in the terms of its own OFW.

The first option, that of bringing the Entity into the parent Framework seems fraught with problems. First, there is the question of identity. Given that an Entity is what it is because it is that particular entity, and thus a particular kind of Entity, it does not appear that its identity could be maintained if an Entity in one framework ceased to be in its own framework and began to be in another. It would no longer be itself, as being itself seems to entail being exactly that particular entity in that framework. In philosophical terms, this would involve changing the nature or essence of the object. Furthermore, we might ask what exactly would be the continuity between an Entity in the Dependent OFW and the new Entity in the Foundational OFW. What would be the same about it?

We might perhaps theorize that bringing the Entity in the Dependent OFW into our OFW simply meant something like putting cameras up in our world and allowing the data of those images to come to a subjective conscious Entity in the Dependent OFW. We could speak to the entity, and show it our world. However, what this really means is the translation of data from our world into the terms of the data of the Dependent OFW. Unless this were the case, the Entity in the Dependent OFW would not be able to receive the video or audio that we give it. This actually equates to the second of our two options.

This second option, communicating with the Entities in the Dependent OFW on their own terms, seems to be the only possible way of communication that guarantees their continued identity. Our communication must be accommodated to the Dependent OFW so that it has the ability to function there as communication. Yelling at my video game avatar, no matter how loud, does not communicate to it that I want it to duck when a fireball is coming its way. Only when I communicate in ways that the game can properly receive is my communication meaningful and efficacious in the Dependent OFW.

Now there are a number of ramifications to this observation. The first is that, given that all communication from the Foundational OFW to the Dependent OFW must be on the terms of the Dependent OFW, all communication will be insufficient to truly express the thought behind the communication. As above, all terms and concepts into which the intended communication will be insufficient for the expression of the realities of the Foundational OFW.

Second, because all communication between the two OFWs must be in the terms of each OFW respectively, each will appear natural to the other. A communication to a world that receives XML data as a mode of communication will receive XML Data "naturally" on its own terms. The cause of the XML might be supernatural, but there will be nothing "supernatural" about the XML Data itself. A world that receives communication by sound may hear a voice from the sky. The source of the voice might be supernatural, but the sound itself will be perfectly natural.[32]

Third, because of this, there can be no evidential proof that the events are supernatural in nature and thus can be doubted. Not originating in the systematic processes of the OFW, they also will not be repeatable and thus not testable. Instead, they will appear merely as unexplained phenomena.

From the Christian perspective, this explains a significant amount regarding the phenomena of miracles in the history of humanity. It also gives us some perspective on the interaction between all supernatural agents, such as angels, and our own world. People hear voices because we receive communication by sound. People see visions because we are visual creatures. We feel a twinge of conscience because that is how we know things are right and wrong. If we are being interacted with by outside supernatural powers, they would and must appear as natural occurrences that can be doubted. But we must also therefore see why they could be doubtable, and that they could not be anything but if the basic Christian distinction between God and the world is true.[33]

Eschatology

With the exceptions of the virtual worlds running at the moment you are reading this, all virtual worlds that have ever existed have ended. The vast majority have come to their ends without any pomp or circumstance. None, as far as I am aware, have achieved a fulfillment that might offer their Entities what we might call eternal life. In other words, their realities have not been assured and fulfilled in a permanent and meaningful way.

Yet, this is the promise of Christianity, that not only will each person come to some eternal state of being, but that the whole world will be made new. The question, with regard to OFWs is one that seems to point us to the question of linking a Dependent OFW to the Foundational OFW in a way that blurs the line between the two.

Our model, a game of *The Elder Scrolls*, affords us little help here.[34] So much of eschatological work is the work of the imaginative faculty.[35] We might ask what a full eschatology in the Christian sense might be for a subjective conscious Entity in a future version of *The Elder Scrolls*. The end of the game world for that subjective Entity would mean the end of its own existence, with no guarantor of identity to come in the future.

Only by more fully linking the game world to our own, by tying its reality to our own, might we give what semblance of an eschatological reality to that world we are capable of offering.

However, due to the fact that a Dependent OFW is tied to its Foundational OFW, it follows that the ultimate fate of the Dependent OFW is linked to the fate of the Foundational OFW. It is clear that a Foundational OFW can terminate a Dependent OFW without intrinsic harm to itself. However, it cannot offer continued existence to a Dependent OFW, if its own existence is discontinued or its ability to sustain a Dependent OFW is discontinued.

Therefore in our own OFW, we find that the only actual eschatological hope that we can offer a dependent OFW is tied to our own eschatological hope. Given the eventual death of the universe as we know it, either through a "big-crunch" or the more currently prevailing perspective of eventual heat-death, our OFW's ability to sustain Dependent OFWs is limited chronologically. There will come a point at which the power and complexity necessary to sustain such OFWs, as we can, will no longer be available. Only if our universe itself is eschatologically renewed and maintained can any real eschatological reality be offered to our Dependent OFWs.

Thus we find that, as with each area we have considered above, Dependent OFWs rely fully on their Foundational OFWs for their entire make up.

Trinitarian Theology

The theory of the OFW also applies to the ontological questions of the Trinity. Recent attempts to "flatten" the Trinitarian hierarchy into what we might call a "extreme perichoresis" have sought to make the three persons or hypostases of the Trinity totally mutually dependent. In this model, the Father, Son and Spirit each depend on each other, with no order of procession that might indicate priority. The admirable goal of such models is to create a model of divine life which gives grounds for equality and mutuality that humanity can emulate. If God is equal, then humanity may be equal.

Kathryn Tanner's insight that it is not the Trinity, but the Incarnation, that gives us a model for lived Christian life is worth repeating. The Trinitarian Hierarchy is not given as a model for exact point by point emulation in human life. Instead, the lived life of Jesus of Nazareth, the anointed, crucified and raised One of God, is.

But there is another fundamental problem with a model of the Trinity which relies on this extreme perichoresis. In the traditional model in which the Father begets the Son and Spirit, the relationship between the Father, Son and Spirit is clearly rooted in the Father's being *(fons divinitatis)*. When we ask what the context for the relationship of the Three Persons' is, we may say either "the Father" if we hold to the Eastern understanding of procession. If we hold to the traditional western reading of the processions, the Father is the context for the Son, and the Father and Son are the context for the Spirit.

But in a model of extreme perichoresis, we must ask what the context or OFW for the three hypostases is. What is the mode of relationship? In what way do they have relationship with each other, or what reality is the context that allows them to relate to each other? If the Father is not the origin, the source of the other two persons, then what is? We may not answer that it is the divine nature, for that will bring about the dreaded "fourth thing" in the Trinity on which the West is often (perhaps incorrectly) accused of relying. Nature, in the sense of the divine nature, is not a context, but an abstracted description.

Thus, looking through the lens of the proposed Theory, we can see that for there to be relations between the three hypostases , they must exist in the same OFW. For the traditional model, that OFW is the Father who shares His whole being with the Son and Spirit. In the "flat" model of the Trinity, we must introduce an OFW external to the Trinity that allowa the three Hypostases to be in relation.

CONCLUSION

All examinations are biased by those who begin them. This consideration of a metaphysic of Ontological Frameworks is attempted in the hope of an honest and empirical observation. However, in that it lines up so closely with Christian theological tradition, it invites critique and criticism. Such critique and criticism is indeed invited and expected given the relative youth of such philosophical and theological considerations of the new virtual worlds we can bring about through computers.

Yet, this proposal also hopes to set some clear boundaries as to how we can speak about Ontological Frameworks with regard to virtual worlds and to God's relationship with our world. It is the author's hope that by clearly defining these relationships, we may both reconsider older problems, such as the supernatural, the revelatory and the natural, as well as newer problems such as artificial intelligence.

Finally, with the advent of such ubiquitous technology, it is hoped that such a theory will allow the use of that technology to work as a ready analogy for the teaching of Christian doctrine in ways that are relevant and helpful. It may not be easy to communicate to a student exactly why Apollinaris' concept of the *tautokinetos* of Christ was wrong. But if the concept of a *tautokinetos* is shown to be similar to that of my character in *Oblivion* . . . we may have a much easier time of teaching the right doctrine instead.

WORKS CITED

Bauckham, Richard. *The Oxford Handbook of Systematic Theology.* "Eschatology". New York: Oxford University Press, 2010, 306-322.

Hawking, Stephen and Mlodinow, Leonard. *The Grand Design.* New York: Bantam Books, 2010.

Huizinga , Johan. *Homo Ludens.* Boston: Beacon Press, 1955.

Krauss, Lawrence M. *A Universe From Nothing: Why there is Something Rather than Nothing.* New York: Free Press, 2012.

Lewis, Clive Staples. *Miracles: A Preliminary Study.* San Francisco, HarperCollins, 2001.

Lewis, Clive Staples. *Out of the Silent Planet.* New York, Scribner Paperback Fiction, 1996.

Sokolowski, Robert. *The God of Faith and Reason: Foundations of Christian Theology.* Washington, D.C.: The Catholic University of America Press, 1995.

Schut, Kevin. *Of Games and God.* Grand Rapids, Brazos Press, 2013.

Wagner, Rachel. "God in the Game: Cosmopolitanism and Religious Conflict in Videogames." *Journal of the American Academy of Religion* 81, no. 1 (March 2013): 249-261

Walls, Jerry L. *Purgatory: The Logic of Total Transformation.* New York: Oxford University Press, 2012.

Endnotes

[1] This essay builds on and shares some common material with my article on Ontological Framework on OntologicalGeek (*http://ontologicalgeek.com/an-empirical-metaphysic-theology-and-virtual-worlds/*)

[2] I attribute this particular observation to my former professor Dr. Timothy Wengert.

[3] It should here be admitted that at least one inspiration for this model comes from a technical source, Microsoft's .net framework. The model, which establishes an existing layer of communication between the operating system, and a layer which communicates with the written code of a program, allows for modular layers that can be adapted for each environment in which the program might be run. There is no attempt here at a one to one comparison between the models, but the general structure of the idea is related. Non technological

versions of this technique, however, have been present since the very beginning of the preaching of the Gospel, as seen in Paul's adaptation of the unknown God in Acts 17.

[4] Self contained here should not be confused for self-existent or self-sustaining.

[5] Either term could have been used here. The concept of an entity or existent, however, is used to include more than what would generally be included in the terminology of "object" or "thing" as there are existents in modern physics, such as fields, which it appears are not to be considered as "objects" or "things" and yet remain as existents.

[6] There are significant questions as to whether or not this is even conceptually possible. Current debates regarding the continuity of identity in Eschatology reflect these concerns, as well as some of the fundamental questions of theosis. For an introduction to this discussion, see Jerry L. Walls, *Purgatory: The Logic of Total Transformation* (New York: Oxford University Press, 2012), p. 99-122.

[7] An example of this might be that transistors in our world actually take part in bringing about transistors in a virtual world. The transistors in the virtual world would only be analogously the same kind of thing as the transistors in our world, as the definition of what a transistor is in our world assumes the structure of our world. The definition of a transistor in a virtual world would assume the structure of that world. What is analogously the same would most likely be function, though perhaps form might come into the analogy as well.

[8] Fields, which are a topic of modern debate in the field of physics, are not themselves considered objects, and thus do not seem to fall under this statement. However, while they may not be objects, they would, if they exist within our framework, and have mutually potential causality with objects, would be considered entities in our OFW. However, if they do not have mutually potential causality, they would be considered to be entities of another OFW functioning either in a sibling relationship, or as part of a possible foundational OFW to our own. This seems to fit with some theories put forward suggesting a possible monochromatic electromagnetic field that underlies our universe' existence. (*http://www.csicop.org/sb/show/ why_is_there_something_rather_than_nothing*).

[9] We are also not here concerned with the question of where the Fictional World definitively begins and ends. It may be useful (as in Michael's essay) to consider the extended fiction for discussion purposes, or to reign in the material (as in my other essay) to the "official" published material. Whichever is chosen, it remains the Fictional World.

[10] Thus, while there may be "remnants" of the program in memory (blocks of memory which no longer are being used for the virtualization of the OFW, but which have not yet been overwritten by new data), the world does not exist in a lesser ontological state. Instead, the world simply ceases to exist as a dependent OFW as the dependent OFW is not merely a collection of component parts, but a relational reality that emerges from our reality and comes to be only when those relational elements are existent together. The data that remains is meaningless without its context, and thus different than say the remains of a building which still partially stand.

[11] Here we are using generic class terms, not supposing these are the actual class names defined in the code of the game.

[12] We will turn to the analogy of OFW in the Epistemology section.

[13] The most common instance of this interaction between instances of the same game would probably be the game's save-file.

[14] This theory is not contradicted by a proposal that the universe springs forth from a field, as some contemporary theories propose. The field, being the condition for the universe, would in fact be considered part of the creation that God brings forth in the free act of creation. This is no more of a hurdle than saying that the sub-atomic particles that are necessary to make up atoms were brought forth into being in order to bring about the complex molecules that make up bread or wine.

[15] Consider St. Anselm's discussion in *Monologion 19* as well as more recently Laurence Krauss's plea that he can't pin theologians down by what they mean by "nothing." Krauss, Lawrence, *A Universe From Nothing: Why there is Something Rather than Nothing* (New York: Free Press, 2012). The human mind, consummately naming and categorizing things, has often categorized "nothing" as a thing. This brings about only confusion as "nothing" is exactly non-entity, and being non-entity can have no attributes, including the ability to be categorized. The fact that the last sentence is itself self-contradictory, since "not being able to be categorized" is itself an attempt at categorization, shows how impossible it is for the human mind to grasp nothing. A perhaps apt example in modern computing will give some sense at how empty "nothing" really is. In certain kinds of databases, the default value for fields is "NULL". "NULL" is a non-value that cells have before anything is every placed in them. NULL, being a non-value, is neither greater nor less than any other value, and always returns false if compared with another value for equality. This is not only true for values, such as numbers or words, but also for other "NULL" fields. NULL does not even equal NULL because it cannot be compared. This gives some idea of the total non-entity that we mean when we theologians say "nothing".

One then finds that one must distinguish between the concept of "nothing" and the "reality". However, the reality is a non-existent, and thus ultimately cannot be linked to the concept. The concept then links to no reality at all, but in a special way that, for example, the concept of a unicorn does not. Thus we see the impossibility of defining "nothing" and the problems associated with any discussion surrounding it. Therefore the phrase "creation from no prior reality" will be used to avoid these complications.

[16] "At once" here is used as only an approximation. If time is one of the things that God brings into being, then we must not conceive of the creation of time as itself temporal. Instead, given point 6 from above, we must conclude that the relationship between time and eternity is defined by eternity, and is thus, at least on some level, an eternal relationship. It would seem nonsense to say that the relationship between time, which is derived, and eternity, which is foundational, is defined by time.

[17] Once more, modern physics is no bar to this. The fact that it seems that the early moments of the universe gave rise to the laws of physics as we know them does not contradict this. There must have been some kinds of laws in existence that dictated how the first moments transpired, and in what way they would bring about the laws of physics as we have them now. Otherwise, without any laws or attributes for each entity to conform to, nothing at all would have happened, for there would have been no defined way for the entities at the beginning of the universe to interact in order to bring about the laws of physics.

[18] This has been expressed another way by the Aristotelian observation that like begets like, and that a product reflects its maker.

[19] Rahner, Karl, *Foundations of Christian Faith: An Introduction to the Idea of Christianity* (New York: Crossroad, 1992).

[20] We take here as evident that the term "supernatural" can be applied to interactions that come from the Foundational OFW into the Dependent OFW. These interactions need not originate only in the Foundational OFW, and may come either from another Dependent OFW, or even an OFW that is Foundational to the Foundational OFW in question. As per attribute 5 above, any interaction with the Dependent OFW will come through the Foundational OFW. Thus, supernatural interactions may originate in many different OFWs, but ultimately come into contact with a particular OFW either directly (interaction from Dependent OFW to Parent OFW) or by the medium of the immediately Foundational OFW to the Dependent OFW in question. Supernatural interaction then encompasses all interactions with an OFW which originate from outside of their own OFW. This, however, does not include interactions between a Dependent OFW and its Foundational OFW, for the Dependent OFW is included in the Foundational OFW's make up.

21 C.S. Lewis, in his book *Miracles*, demonstrates this elegantly. The fact that we can observe his descriptions in virtual worlds now shows that his logic was sound. C.S. Lewis, *Miracles: A Preliminary Study*, (San Francisco, HarperCollins, 2001).

[22] Stephen Hawking and Leonard Mlodinow, *The Grand Design*, (New York: Bantam Books, 2010), 5-10.

[23] Thus, Schut, is right in saying that killing a character in a game is not the same as killing a real person. Within the context of the distinction of the Foundational and Dependent OFW's, there is no real comparison between a digital character and a real person. However, even in the context of the player's perception, the character exists in the context of the world as understood by meaning 3 above, the fiction he or she perceives as fiction. Kevin Schut, *Of Games and God* (Grand Rapids, Brazos Press, 2013).

[24] Here we are not particularly considering the effects that changes in data can have on real life situations like the manipulation of data that people depend on, like bank accounts, or the stock market. Our question is located purely in the observation and imparting of meaning to virtual worlds by people in our own OFW.

[25] It is here that we must disagree with Paul Fiddes with regard to his stance on Communion and Second Life (http://www.docstoc.com/docs/86883542/virtual-communion). The "logic" of any virtual world that would allow for the avatar to receive grace exists purely in the second and third meaning of the virtual world that we have given above. An avatar no more receives grace by the change in one specific attribute (HasReceivedCommunionToday = True) than in another (XLocation = 1150). Only in the fiction that we attach to a world, in the world that we create in our own heads, or in our subjective experience is meaning or grace expressed. Each of these levels of meaning, it must be noted, exist in our own world, not in the dependent OFW.

The "logic of Second Life" is a logic that exists, not in the game of Second life, but in our own world. As observed above, the rules of any Dependent OFW are defined by the Foundational OFW which hosts it. Thus, Fiddes' view that grace is conveyed to avatars is true in the sense that avatars, qua avatars, exist as constructs in our world that are a meta reality for the actual OFW that Second Life is.

A simple test helps us to see this. The first considers the avatar without a player behind it acting out the same actions when "receiving communion" as it would if the player was behind it. Is there any reason to expect that grace is conveyed in that reality to objects which have no subjectivity by which they can receive the grace? What makes the action of "receiving communion" distinct from the change of hair color in that world? They are both simple changes in state in the object within the software.

It is only by our addition of meaning to the virtual world that it has any meaning at all. We may, then, ask whether or not the virtual communion has meaning because we give it meaning, or if grace is conveyed to the person controlling the game *ex opere operantis*. That may be, but this would then bring about questions regarding valid Eucharist or Communion, in general, that are beyond the scope of this essay.

[26] The supposed value of First-Person shooters, not here addressed, as binary structures which guarantee moral certitude, as proposed by Rachel Wagner in "God in the Game: Cosmopolitanism and Religious Conflict in Videogames," *Journal of the American Academy of Religion* 81, No. 1 (March 2013): 249-261, is highly questionable. However, the question is pertinent here as Wagner's "survey" of video games is so limited that it fails to encompass large open world that also contain violence, such as *Mass Effect* and specifically here, *The Elder Scrolls*. While Wagner does address *World of Warcraft*, her assessment of it is so surface level as to not address the actual interactions of players who collaborate together to accomplish strategic and tactical goals. She as well attests that in-game bigotries (Orc vs. Humans, etc.) can lead to real-world bigotries without any substantiating evidence. The argument made in the article, that a Cosmopolitan view of the world is needed, but not essentially possible in video games, is belied by the depths of meaning and cultural relativity that are evidenced in the meaning that a series like *The Elder Scrolls*, or *Mass Effect*, are imbued with by the creators and players of these games. (There are numerous other problems with Wagner's assessment of video games and violence that are not here relevant, but deserve fuller treatment at a later point).

[27] This is distinct from John Huizinga's concept of the "Magic Circle" in which games are played, but has something of the same result. Our interaction with Dependent OFWs, when in the state of play, may in fact involve entering the Magic Circle in which the rules are quite different. However, I would argue that the act of "killing" which is permitted in the magical circle, is merely analogous. The act of killing is allowed because it is killing only on the level of the Dependent OFW, and therefore does not retain the value of the analogous act in the Foundational OFW. See Johan Huizinga, *Homo Ludens* (Boston: Beacon Press, 1955).

[28] The reference here to Edwin Abbot's seminal *Flatland* is of course noted.

[29] Or even, in fact, if in creating the interpretive layer for the Nerevarine of his own world, we did not build it so that it represented his world to him in the same way we see it. Because the underlying reality is data which is represented as mountains, rivers, and houses, any interpretive layer put on top of that data need not represent it in the same way that it has been represented to us through our media devices. A rather humorous example may be found by looking at the modding community in gaming which can easily replace default models in games with sometimes ridiculous replacements. But we may go even further to suggest that even the three-dimensional world that is virtualized for us need not be the only way in which the data represented by x,y,z integers can be understood.

[30] We could, for example, program an entity to observe only the attributes of an object, and derive relationships from those attributes. Or we could allow an object to only be aware of other objects with particular attributes given a set of rules. This is more like how actual AI routines work in games.

[31] Dependent OFW's that share a common Foundational OFW are somewhat different. For example, it seems fair to say that two instances of the same virtual world have entities in them that stand or act in the same ways that are actually the same, and not merely analogous. Of course, this need not be the case. Daggerfall and Pac-Man are, for the purposes of this discussion, nothing alike.

[32] This results in a very interesting mode of communication between Dependent OFWs that have a common Foundational OFW. By a union only possible through their Foundational OFW, two "sibling" OFW's (OFW A, and OFW B) might interact with each other. All of OFW A's actions will be natural to it, and the effects of its actions will be natural in its own OFW. However, by the union created by the Foundational OFW, there will be effects in OFW B. These will be natural effects with a "supernatural" cause, due to the fact that the OFW that caused them was not itself. Thus, in the test-case of angels, an angelic action, in its own OFW, may result, if God grants it, in effects in our OFW. However, not only will the angel be supernatural to us, but we will be supernatural to it. C.S. Lewis predicted this to some great degree in his space trilogy, C.S. Lewis, *Out of the Silent Planet*, (New York: Scribner Paperback Fiction, 1996), p. 119-120.

[33] Robert Sokolowski, *The God of Faith and Reason: Foundations of Christian Theology*, (Washington, D.C.: The Catholic University of America Press, 1995).

[34] For what help it can offer, see Jacob Torbeck's essay in this book.

[35] Richard Bauckham, *The Oxford Handbook of Systematic Theology*, "Eschatology", (New York: Oxford University Press, 2010), 316-318.

Biographies

Matthew Franks is a PhD student at Catholic University of America's School of Theology (Religion and Culture). He received his Master of Theological Studies at Boston University and his B.A. in Philosophy and Religion from Hendrix College. His research interests center on the interconnections of religion, politics, and art.

Recent publications include an article on religion and National Socialism in Harvard's graduate journal Cult/ure, and his fiction has appeared in Zahir and the The Arkansas Literary Forum under the pen name Gibson Monk.

Joshua Gonnerman lives in Washington, DC, where he is pursuing a doctorate in historical theology at the Catholic University of America. His main area of research in Augustine of Hippo.

Mark Hayse is Professor of Christian Education and Director of the Honors Program at MidAmerica Nazarene University in Olathe, Kansas. His publications on video games include "Ultima IV: Simulating the Religious Quest" in Halos and Avatars: Playing Video Games with God (2010, Westminster/John Knox), "The Mediation of Transcendence within The Legend of Zelda: The Wind Waker" in The Legend of Zelda and Theology(2011, Gray Matter Books), entries in Don't Stop Believin' : Pop Culture and Religion from Ben-Hur to Zombies (2012, Westminster/ John Knox), entries in the Encyclopedia of Video Games: The Culture, Technology, and Art of Gaming (2012, Greenwood), and entries in the Routledge Companion to Video Game Studies (forthcoming, Routledge). His research interests lie at the intersection of curriculum theory, theology, and ludology.

Jacob W. Torbeck is a husband, father, fantasy geek, Lay Dominican, and an adjunct professor of theology at Holy Apostles College and Seminary. When he isn't actively attempting to master being a husband and father, his research interests fall in the areas of systematic and philosophical theology, especially where these converge upon issues of self and identity.

Joshua Wise is a Doctoral Student of Systematic Theology at Catholic University of America. He is the host of the podcast No Avatars Allowed, and editor of the Website www.CrossedPurposes.com. His main area of study is Christocentric Eschatology.

Michael Zeigler received his Master of Arts in Religion from Lancaster Theological Seminary. He lives in Central Pennsylvania with his wife Karin and their eight (!) cats.

CPSIA information can be obtained
at www.ICGtesting.com
Printed in the USA
FFOW03n2105150915
16807FF